PREACHING
THROUGH THE
PROPHETS

John B. Taylor

Bishop of St Albans

CBP Press

St. Louis, Missouri

Copyright © John B. Taylor, 1983

First published 1983
by A. R. MOWBRAY & CO LTD
SAINT THOMAS HOUSE, BECKET STREET,
OXFORD OX1 1SJ

Scripture quotations, unless otherwise noted, are from the Revised Standard Version of the Bible, copyrighted 1946, 1952, C 1971, 1973 by the Division of Christian Education of the National Council of the Churches of Christ in the U.S.A. and are used by permission.

Library of Congress Cataloging in Publication Data

Taylor, John Bernard.
    Preaching through the prophets.

    1. Bible. O.T. Prophets—Sermons—Outlines, syllabi, etc.   2. Sermons—Outlines, syllabi, etc.   I. Title.
BS1505.4.T39 1985   251'.02   84-23773
ISBN 0-8272-2929-1

ISBN: 0-8272-2929-1

Printed in the United States of America

CONTENTS

INTRODUCTION

This is not a book of sermons. It is a collection of sermon-outlines, providing the framework around which other people's sermons may be built. There is a deliberate lack of polish, because I have not wanted anyone to think that these are finished products which can be served up straight from the pot. So illustrations are few and application is sparse, for these are elements which must be the preacher's own and suited to the occasion.

I take the view that a sermon is a meeting-place between a preacher and a congregation, a magnetic field in which all kinds of unseen forces are at work between those two poles, and every sermon is unique and unrepeatable. By this I do not mean that material cannot be used over again, simply that it must come across as today's message for today's congregation. If it fails to do that, it fails to be the word of God; it is merely a homily, a spoken essay.

Preaching from the prophets means the bridging of an enormous gap two thousand five hundred years wide. On the one hand we must be faithful to the prophet's original context and meaning, and yet attempt to bring his words home with force and authority to twentieth century westerners. Some who read these outlines will think that they would be safer to stick to the Gospels. I hope they will resist the temptation to do so and persist in the effort to make the Old Testament prophets come alive for the Christians of today. For here are thirty first-class texts that cry out for exposition and application. If I have not done them justice (and I am all too conscious of the fact), I would like to derive comfort from the thought that I may have spurred my readers to do it better, in their way.

Almost all of these outlines have been preached by me at some time or another over the past ten years, though I doubt if anyone will remember having heard them. No one who borrows and adapts them need feel at all inhibited thereby.

The hymns have been selected mainly from *Ancient and Modern Revised* and from *100 Hymns for Today* and the biblical quotations are in general from RSV. I should like to express my thanks to Mrs Audrey Glydon for typing the manuscript and to

the publishers for their patience in extending deadlines in order
to allow me time to settle into my new job.

Abbey Gate House †JOHN ST ALBANS
St Albans
1982

1. HEAR THE WORD OF THE LORD

Isaiah 1. 2,3 *'Hear, O heavens, and give ear, O earth; for the Lord has spoken: "Sons have I reared and brought up, but they have rebelled against me. The ox knows it owner, and the ass its master's crib; but Israel does not know, my people does not understand".'*

Aim: To give an introduction to Isaiah's prophecy and to the main themes of the Old Testament prophets as a whole. Read Isaiah 1. 1–20 for the first lesson.

The story has been reported from Israel of an incident involving the Israeli police depot at Beersheba. A police patrol had intercepted a band of Arab smugglers crossing the Negev desert from Egyptian to Jordanian territory. The Bedouin escaped but the goods and the camels and mules were captured. One alert police sergeant suspected that the wrongdoers might possibly be based in an encampment on his side of the frontier line, so he devised this simple strategem to catch them. Several of the mules were kept in police custody and starved of food for three days. They were then allowed to go free and driven off into the desert. Instinct and hunger did the rest, and they obligingly led the police straight back to their owners' tents. The ox knows its owner, and the ass its master's crib. It does indeed.

The Old Testament prophets had a rare gift for that kind of vivid home truth. They did not simply tell people that they were wicked. They said 'Your hands are full of blood'. Not that they were hypocrites, but, 'Your righteousness is like a filthy rag'.

Isaiah was a pastmaster at this kind of prophecy, and here in the first chapter of his book we are given a selection of his favourite themes. The chapter is an introduction not only to his own prophecy but to the whole line of prophets from Amos to Malachi. Each had his own distinctive message but the standpoint of them all was the same, and it was a case of variations on a limited number of themes. Here are some of them.

1. *The nation's troubles are more serious than people appreciate*

It was the prophet's duty to challenge the people along with their rulers and clergy, and to remind them of the requirements of the old covenant dating back to Moses on Mount Sinai. Israel

1

was a nation especially chosen by God, miraculously delivered at the crossing of the Red Sea, destined to bear witness to God's truth and holiness, expected to live at least by the standards of the Ten Commandments and to have a morality noticeably higher than her neighbours round about. They were to preserve their faith intact, they were not to trifle with idolatry of any kind, and they were to be unswerving in their loyalty to the Lord and to none else.

But they did not keep it up. Instead, they made matters worse by pretending that nothing was seriously wrong. They made great play with their privileges – a chosen people, children of Abraham, heirs of God's promises, and so forth – but they paid little attention to the conditions that were imposed.

So Isaiah tells them that they are rotten through and through. 'The whole head is sick, the whole heart faint. From the sole of the foot even to the head, there is no soundness in it, but bruises and sores and bleeding wounds . . .' (1.5,6). Instead of belonging to the Lord, they have forsaken him; instead of honouring his name 'they have despised the Holy One of Israel, they are utterly estranged' (1.4). Only by grasping the truth of statements like these will God's people stand a chance of seeming any change of fortune. The first step on the way back to God – for the nation as well as for the individual – is to echo the words of the prodigal son. 'Father I have sinned against heaven and before you; I am no longer worthy to be called your son.'

2. *Religion without morality is anathema to God*

'What to me is the multitude of your sacrifices? says the Lord; I have had enough of burnt offerings of rams and the fat of fed beasts. . . . Bring no more vain offerings; incense is an abomination to me. . . Your new moons and your appointed feasts my soul hates; they have become a burden to me, I am weary of bearing them' (1.11–14).

Now, this is strong language, so much so that some have argued that Isaiah and the prophets stood for a religion of personal and social morality to the exclusion of the established worship of temple and sacrifices. But that is going too far. After all, some of the prophets were actually on the staff of the temple or were trained to the priesthood, so it would be unthinkable to turn them into opponents of the very religion which the law of

Moses ordered to be observed. No, their criticisms were harsh, but they carried weight because they were uttered from within organised religion, not from outside it. What they were pleading for was a quality of life and conduct which was acceptable to God, to match the offerings and sacrifices being made to him. Religion without morality just would not do.

3. *A change of heart and a change of direction are needed*

The New Testament word is repentance, but in the prophets the commonest word is simply to turn or to return. Isaiah does not use that word in this chapter, but instead, in verses 16–20, he gives a brief summary of what is meant by it.

First comes renouncing evil: 'wash yourselves; make yourselves clean; remove the evil of your doings from before by eyes'. Now it is abundantly clear that the sinner cannot make himself clean; only God can do that. But the sinner can and must wash his hands of his sins and turn his back on them. He has to let go of them if he is going to turn to God.

Then comes a new determination: 'cease to do evil, learn to do good; seek justice, correct oppression; defend the fatherless, plead for the widow.' Again this is not salvation by self-improvement, but it does mean that the man who turns to God must realise what he is turning to – a life of holy, responsible behaviour, caring for goodness and concerned for people's needs. All this is contained in the baptismal promise, 'I turn to Christ'. Every Christian should be both a good neighbour and a social reformer.

Finally there comes the essential element of choice and decision. 'Come now, let us reason together, says the Lord: though your sins are like scarlet, they shall be as white as snow; though they are red like crimson, they shall become like wool. If you are willing and obedient. . .' (1.18,19). The possibility of forgiveness is always held out to sinful man by the prophets, but it is a possibility and not a guarantee. Man must be willing and decide to return to God. Only then will judgement turn to blessing and God's wrath give way to God's favour.

It is not a long step from the preaching of an Isaiah to the call of the evangelist today. Both are seeking to catch the ear of contemporary man and to speak the truth as they find it. Both are recalling the nation to standards long since abandoned and to a better quality of life. Both are saying that it is only be an encounter with the living God that man can find the grace to be forgiven and to become a new person in Christ. This is the message of the prophets, whether they live in the eighth century before Christ or in the twentieth century after him.

Prayer: Open our ears, Lord, to hear your word and to lay it seriously to heart. Open our eyes, Lord, to see its truth with greater clarity. Open our hearts, Lord, that we may turn to you and give ourselves without reserve, and then live accordingly.

(Hymns: Come, let us to the Lord our God; A safe stronghold our God is still; God is working his purpose out.)

2. SOUR GRAPES

Isaiah 5,7 *'The vineyard of the Lord of hosts is the house of Israel, and the men of Judah are his pleasant planting; and he looked for justice, but behold, bloodshed; for righteousness, but behold, a cry!'*

Aim: To illustrate how the prophets could use the commonplace as a vehicle for communicating God's word. Read Isaiah 5. 1–16 for the first lesson.

It needs little imagination to see this passage in its original context. It reads like open-air preaching at its very best. A speaker, a story, a crowd, a roar of support and then the body-blow. 'The vineyard of the Lord of hosts is the house of Israel.' Let me fill in the background.

The setting would have been the Feast of Tabernacles towards the end of the Israelite summer. It was a kind of harvest festival, but with particular reference to the grape harvest, the vintage. During the week-long festivities, religious attractions in Jerusalem would have been mingled with carousing in the streets and late night drinking sessions by the young and the indisciplined. The tradition of sleeping out under the stars in 'booths' or shelters as a reminder of Israel's pilgrimage from Egypt must have been observed by many inebriated Israelites out of helpless necessity rather than from religious conviction. Yes, Tabernacles was a great festival but it had its problems. It was not by accident that later Judaism chose to read the little book of Ecclesiastes every year at Tabernacles, to remind people of the vanity of life and to sober them up.

Now that is not the easiest situation for heavy preaching. But Isaiah caught the spirit of the occasion first – always a good principle to adopt if one is going to have the remotest chance of being listened to. He picked a place where the people congregated naturally and began to speak. They had time to listen and he had a story to tell: a love song about a young man and his vineyard. 'My beloved had a vineyard on a very fertile hill.'

The timing is good, the lyrics strike a familiar chord and the curiosity is aroused. It soon transpires that the speaker is actually the owner of the vineyard, but the hearers don't notice the transition. What do I do with a vineyard into which I have put so much effort and care? What has gone wrong with it that the crop turns out to be sour grapes and not sweet ones? It sounds a little like 'Gardeners' Question Time', but Isaiah does not pretend to be the expert. He plays the role of ingenuous questioner. The audience becomes the panel, and no doubt it was free with its advice. Plant new stock – dig in more compost – prune the roots hard. But the prophet has made up his mind. He is going to destroy his own handiwork, lay waste the land, render it useless and derelict for ever – and at once the hint of a parable begins to shine through the story. 'The vineyard of the Lord of hosts is the house of Israel, and the men of Judah are his pleasant planting.'

Israel's sour grapes were oppression instead of justice and the crying of people trodden down when they should have been given a helping hand. Isaiah used a play on words to get this home. God was looking for righteousness (*tsedaqah*), and all he found was an outcry (*tse'aqah*). The first word meant good government, honesty in public life, concern for the underprivileged, a fair deal for all. The second meant a cry of distress, anguish, oppression. It was the word used in Genesis 18. 20: "The *outcry* against Sodom and Gomorrah is great and their sin is very grave', and in Exodus 3.7: 'I have seen the affliction of my people who are in Egypt, and have heard their *cry* because of their taskmasters.' In a word, Isaiah was saying that Judah compared unfavourably with Egypt and with Sodom and Gomorrah, those bywords for unbelief and barbarism.

Having gained a hearing and made his point, Isaiah needed to justify and elaborate these charges. He did it in the form of a series of six 'Woes' (verses 8, 11, 18, 20, 21, 22). They are not a complete list, but if they are at all typical they show the kinds of sin that called down the prophet's anger. Let us look at a few of them.

1. The greed of the land-grabber

'Woe to those who join house to house, who add field to field, until there is no more room, and you are made to dwell alone in the midst of the land.' When the ownership of a strip of land was the Israelite's sole guarantee of independence and a livelihood for himself and his family, the acquisitiveness of the land grabber was a particularly heartless crime. The way it was done was wrong – usually by loaning a neighbour money when he fell on hard times or had a poor harvest, and then foreclosing the mortgage and forcing him to sell up. And the results were wrong – large estates whose owners lived in splendid isolation, and the unfortunate victims who lived in serfdom and without hope of betterment.

The prophet pronounces a 'fertility curse' on these feudal upstarts. Their mansions will stand empty and their fields will lose their productivity. 'Ten acres of vineyard shall yield but one bath', a mere four or five gallons of wine; and 'a homer of seed shall yield but an ephah'. That would have raised a laugh if it were not so devastating a curse. It meant that the seed sown would yield not thirtyfold or a hundredfold but *only one tenth* of what was sown. A *ninety per cent* loss! Such was the measure of God's judgement on flagrant exploitation of the land.

It is worth remembering that the Mosaic law insisted that the transfer of land from one owner to another was not permitted. Land was a family's inheritance and it had to remain in family ownership. If for some reason – debt or decease – it passed out of the family, it could only be until the year of jubilee, the half-century mark when all land reverted to its original owner and the *status quo* was restored. So the family had a freehold; anyone else could only obtain a lease of up to forty-nine years.

The message of Isaiah cannot of course be applied directly to modern western society, but the underlying principles are clear. No self-aggrandisement at the cost of another's livelihood is ever acceptable to God. Greed of whatever sort always results in the ultimate downfall of the greedy. God's care takes in the world of national economics as well as of private morality – at some point the two will always intersect.

2. The stupidity of the heavy drinker

'Woe to those who are heroes at drinking wine, and valiant men in mixing strong drink.' It is a pitiable feature of the man who drinks more than is good for him that he hides what is deep down a psychological weakness under a cloak of bravado, and he is for ever asserting his manliness as if to convince himself that he is master of his own will and fully in control of his faculties. The alcoholic has to be very far gone before he admits that he has a problem and will accept help.

Isaiah knew all about this, and so do today's advertisers of beers and spirits. They portray them in the world of fast cars, elegant women and he-man occupations, appealing to the vanity of men who long to be more masculine than they really are. It is the heroism of fools or, to be more charitable, of adolescents.

With the drinking goes the craving – 'Woe to those who rise early in the morning, that they may run after strong drink'. When a man – or a woman for that matter, because alcoholism is no respecter of the sexes – pines for the first drink of the day as soon as he wakes up in the morning, it is a sure sign that he is in the grip of an addiction. He has begun to die. The senses are dulled, the hands tremble, the body runs to seed. The consuming passion is beginning to consume his very life. Such people 'do not regard the deeds of the Lord' because they cannot. They do not 'see the work of his hands' because they have become morally and spiritually blind.

Reclaiming the alcoholic is a task of immense difficulty and success is not often achieved. Reformed alcoholics do not claim to have succeeded in defeating their craving, merely to be succeeding to date. The work of Alcoholics Anonymous is noteworthy in this field and it appears to be increasingly in demand. Meanwhile the Christian's duty is to play his part in warding off the disease before it gets a hold. It is a nettle that the Church is slow to grasp.

3. *The perversity of the moral anarchist*

'Woe to those who call evil good and good evil, who put darkness for light and light for darkness.' This is the topsy-turvydom of those who believe they are entitled to make their own rules in matters of morality and behaviour. It is not far removed from the attitude of those who attributed to the prince of darkness the healing miracles of the Son of God (Mark 3.22–30). This could be what was meant by the blasphemy against the Holy Spirit; certainly something in that class.

All these and many other sins came under the lash of Isaiah's tongue in Jerusalem seven hundred years before Christ. Today the list might differ but the same variety would be there and the words would cut just as deeply. Where are justice and righteousness to be found? And where are we deluding ourselves?

Prayer: Save us, Lord, from the blindness that can see no faults in ourselves but only in other people. Show us where we come short, and give us the grace to change our ways.
(Hymns: We find thee, Lord, in others' need; Rise up, O men of God; The Church of God a kingdom is.)

3. THE VISION IN THE TEMPLE

Isaiah 6.5 *'My eyes have seen the King, the Lord of hosts!'*

Aim: To show the character of God as described in Isaiah's vision, and the consequences for the prophet of that remarkable experience. Isaiah 6 is frequently read on Trinity Sunday but the chapter's theme of call and commission is not to be restricted to that day.

Apart from Saul's conversion on the Damascus road, Isaiah's vision of the Lord on his throne must be the most well-known of all the religious experiences described in the Bible. It comes over to us as a rare piece of spiritual autobiography, as the prophet modestly lets his readers in on the event which was to make an indelible mark on the rest of his life and ministry.

It is interesting to note that this experience is not recorded in chapter 1 of the book. Apparently Isaiah had already embarked on his career as a prophet before this took place. He would not have been allowed into the temple court if he were not already serving in the temple alongside the priests and so able to stand with them in the inner court between the porch and the altar. So religious experience is not restricted to an initial conversion. It can happen at any time along the way.

1. The Lord is King

The opening words of the chapter set the scene. Uzziah the king was dead. He had died of leprosy, contracted (so the story went) as a punishment for invading the very precinct where Isaiah himself was to have his vision. In a moment of big-headedness he had thought that as a king he could do what only priests were allowed to do. His obituary is summed up in the Chronicler's words, 'When he was strong he grew proud, to his destruction' (2 Chr. 26.16). It came as a fearful warning to all the people.

But now he was dead, a long and successful reign ending in a painful and pathetic death. And in the uncertainty of the moment, as Isaiah took part in one of the great festivals of the year, it was as if he saw the Lord as King, sitting upon a throne, high and lifted up. Supreme in the temple, his earthly dwelling-place; supreme in the nation, whose people he ruled; supreme in the events of history, while kings and kingdoms came and went; supreme in his world, for the whole earth was full of his glory.

2. Holy is the Lord

Perhaps it was the circumstances surrounding the dead king's final illness that underlined for Isaiah the Lord's holiness. To be holy means to be separate, distinct, 'untouched by human hand'! In the words of Rudolf Otto, God is 'the Wholly Other One', or as Hosea put it, 'I am God and not man, the Holy One in your midst' (Hosea 11.9). To be *distinct* from man, however, does not mean to be *distant* from man. God is near, but he is also supremely different. This is a hard lesson for man to learn. We like to have a God with whom we can be on friendly terms, and of course God has made himself known to us in Jesus who does actually say that he calls us his friends. But still he is holy, to be worshipped and obeyed. He has indeed come down to earth to be on a par with us, but we are a long way from being on a par with him.

Three times Isaiah repeats the words: 'Holy, holy, holy is the Lord of hosts'. From then onwards his favourite word for God is 'the Holy One of Israel'. Moreover he gives the word a moral content: 'The Lord of hosts is exalted in justice, and the Holy God shows himself holy in righteousness' (5.16). The holiness of God becomes his clarion-call.

Some would say that the Church today needs to recover a sense of God's holiness. I believe they are right. But what would it involve? It would affect our worship most certainly. We would be much more circumspect in making our approach to God, not rushing in like fools but preparing ourselves with thought and prayer. And maybe those long-forgotten disciplines of self-examination before coming to Holy Communion would need to be revived. It would affect our obedience to the moral imperatives of the gospel. Have we, I wonder, hidden behind situational ethics to allow ourselves to go for the moral soft options instead of taking the hard sayings of Christ's teaching more seriously? And what does holiness say about the other-worldly quality of life that strangers and pilgrims on this earth should be cultivating?

3. *A forgiving God*

Isaiah's response to holiness was a feeling of desolation. 'Woe is me! For I am lost; for I am a man of unclean lips, and I dwell in the midst of a people of unclean lips; for my eyes have seen the King, the Lord of hosts!' It reminds me of Peter's reaction to the miraculous draught of fishes, 'Depart from me, for I am a sinful man, O Lord' (Luke 5.8). Yes, even an unexpectedly large catch of fish pointed to Jesus' holiness: he was different, incomparably greater than a Peter or an Andrew. His was a holiness before which you knelt down and confessed your sins.

Holiness does not stand aloof. It stoops down to cleanse and to cauterize. The burning coal taken from the altar fire and pressed to Isaiah's lips is a powerful symbol. It says to us that there is no painless cure for sin. Forgiveness emanates from the place of sacrifice and death, as indeed it does from the Cross, and it does not touch us without our feeling something of the pain and cost of Calvary.

The words spoken by the heavenly messenger reinforced the symbol. 'This has touched your lips; your guilt is taken away, and your sin forgiven.' In that instant Isaiah must have known the enormous relief and release that forgiveness brings. Instead of being separated from God, he now knew himself to be separated from his sin. He was free. Free to serve God, free to speak the word, free to go wherever the Lord should send him.

4. 'Here am I'

In imagination Isaiah hears the Lord discussing with his heavenly advisers the world and its needs. He overhears the question being put, 'Whom shall I send, and who will go for us?' For him there can be no answer but the two words *hinnenî shelaḥēnî*, 'Here am I; send me'. The shortest prayer with the greatest meaning.

This is sometimes described as Isaiah's call. It is not. He was never called. All kinds of things happened to him: he had a vision of God, he was cleansed, but God did not call him. He offered. The 'Whom-shall-I-send' was for the whole world to hear. Isaiah, fired by his experience, leapt forward to offer his service. People who wait to be 'called' before they embark on Christian work will wait in vain. The call is the need. God is always asking his people 'Whom shall I send, and who will go for us?' He is waiting for offers of lives surrendered to his service, made available for him to use.

Then comes the commission: 'Go, and say. . . .' The Christian's commission is similar: 'Go and make disciples of all nations, baptizing them . . . teaching them . . .; and lo, I am with you always, to the end of the age' (Matthew 28.19f.).

We do not have to be people of Isaiah's calibre to share in Isaiah's vision. Our religious experience will be much more modest. But our God is the same, reigning in holiness, forgiving our sins, requiring our service, and we can all listen in on Isaiah's wavelength and be impelled to the same conclusion. Here am I; send me.

Prayer: Open our eyes, Lord, to see you more clearly, that we may be the children of your kingdom and agents of your mission in the world.

(*Hymns: Bright the vision that delighted; Holy, holy, holy, Lord God Almighty; The Lord is king, lift up thy voice; O Jesus, I have promised.*)

4. IMMANUEL, GOD WITH US

Isaiah 7.14 *'Behold, a young woman shall conceive and bear a son, and shall call his name Immanuel.'*

Aim: To clarify the meaning of the virgin prophecy and through it to point to the miracle of the Incarnation. This would be suitable towards the end of Advent or over the Christmas period.

Every year, as Christmas comes round, we prepare to celebrate the birth of the Saviour of the world, Son of Mary and Son of God. We read the gospel stories, we sing the well-loved carols with their strange mixture of scriptural insight and tawdry legend, we find ourselves almost unaccountably caught up in the spirit of goodwill and neighbourliness that affects the whole country for at least three days, and we brace ourselves for the pleasant annual surprise of seeing so many practising unbelievers in church for the Christmas services.

And if our critical faculties have not been dulled by the bombardment of Christmassy noises, greetings and refreshments, we may have time to pause and wonder about the quite preposterous allegation on which Christmas is based. That a virgin should have given birth to a divine Child, begotten of God the Father and conceived by the operation of God the Holy Spirit.

1. *The Virgin Birth*

Those who think that Christmas is an appropriate time to spring to the defence of the virgin birth usually do so in one of two ways. Either they go to this passage in Isaiah and argue about the meaning of the Hebrew word translated 'young woman' or they go to the biological sciences and discuss the evidence for parthenogenesis in other orders of natural life. Both approaches, I submit, are misconceived (if I may use that word in this context).

Natural science can neither accept nor deny the unique manner of our Lord's birth. By definition it deals only with the observable, the verifiable, the repeatable, and Mary's pregnancy falls outside the boundaries of scientific investigation. If it was the unique event the Bible sets it out to be, the scientist can do nothing but shrug his shoulders and admit he has no equipment to assess it with.

Nor does the virgin birth have any dependence on the virgin prophecy of Isaiah 7. Though Matthew described it as the fulfilment of Isaiah's words, it is worth remembering that (a) no Jew ever expected a virgin-born Messiah to appear, and (b) the so-called Immanuel prophecy was not regarded as one of the standard messianic proof-texts that needed to be fulfilled. So at the outset we can clear Matthew, Luke and the rest of the early Church from any suspicion of trying to tell the story to fit the expectations.

The story of Jesus' virgin birth stands upon its own credibility, as reported by the evangelists. Either they told it the way it was, or the way Mary told it to them (there is a good tradition that Luke learnt much from our Lord's mother and the womenfolk) – or they overtold it. We must judge for ourselves. For myself I find it easier to accept that when God chose to reveal himself in a human life, he did it as a one-off exercise rather than go through what bureaucrats call 'the usual channels'. A Saviour of the world, without a touch of the miraculous at the beginning, the middle and the end of his life, I would find totally perplexing.

2. *The circumstances of the prophecy*

But our subject is Isaiah 7 and not the virgin birth and, as we shall see, the link is rather tenuous. If the whole of chapter 7 is read it will be obvious that Isaiah is dealing, not with events seven hundred years into the future, but with a problem that was on his very doorstep. This is what it was. Judah and Israel, her northern neighbour, were frequently sparring with each other but it rarely came to much. This time, however, Israel had found an ally in Syria and a combined invasion force was on the way to Jerusalem. The prospects looked bleak indeed, and Isaiah was commissioned by the Lord to minister to king Ahaz in his hour of danger. This was how the word of the Lord came to him:

'The Lord himself will give you a sign. Behold, a young woman shall conceive and bear a son, and shall call his name Immanuel. He shall eat curds and honey when he knows how to refuse the evil and choose the good. For before the child knows how to refuse the evil and choose the good, the land before whose two kings you are in dread will be deserted' (7.14–16).

The reference to refusing the evil and choosing the good must mean coming to years of discretion. Eating curds and honey is a symbol of pastoral abundance. The fact that a young mother-to-be will be calling her son 'God is with us' indicates that within, say, a twelvemonth there will be that degree of confidence in the air in Judah, in marked contrast to the prevailing mood of pessimism. So the immediate import of the sign is that the tide is turning. Hope in God will soon be back and before many more years are past all will be prosperity and freedom once again.

How then does it tie in with the virgin birth? In two ways. First, because when the Hebrew text was translated into Greek some two hundred years before Christ, the translator rendered the word for 'young woman' by *parthenos*, 'virgin', a meaning the Hebrew can bear but does not demand. And it was not long before the early Christians spotted the word and identified it with the virgin mother of the Christ. Secondly, because with the 'virgin' coincidence there was the incredibly appropriate title of Immanuel, God with us. What better description could there be of God incarnate? Here was clearly a case of Isaiah speaking better than he knew, of the Spirit's inspiration of prophet and translator together to produce a hitherto unrecognized foretelling of the miraculous birth of God's own Son. Beyond that we need not go; but we have already gone far enough to see that Isaiah 7 was quite a remarkable word from God, with one message for the day and another for future generations to listen to and enjoy.

3. *Immanuel*

Finally, let us look again at this name Immanuel. *Im* meaning 'with; *immanu*, 'with us'; immanu-el, 'God with us'. It is the Saviour's name at Christmas, and we sing it or hear it sung a dozen times in our Advent and Christmas anthems. What does it say to us?

We can of course take it and use it as a prayer – 'God be with us'. A pious hope. A kind of *Pax nobiscum*. Maybe that would have suited its original meaning in Isaiah's day. Something tentative and wistful. Why not? If that meaning is to be found anywhere in the word Immanuel, it is surely what we pray for each other this Christmas time. May God be with us, enriching the festivities, hallowing the holiday.

Or we can read it as a theological statement summing up in one word the mind-blowing meaning of the Incarnation. God was in Christ. He has visited and redeemed his people. God has come down to men, to dwell with them and to suffer for them. All this teaching is enshrined in that one word Immanuel – a nutshell that contains a whole world.

Alternatively we can take it as our watchword as we set about our Christmas round of duties and delights. For as we do all these things we can know that God is with us. He is with us as we sign and address those last-minute cards. He is with us as we put up the decorations, prepare the turkey, open our presents and recover on Boxing Day. God is in it all – alongside us, within us, around us. We can neither evade him nor avoid him. He is there.

This should bring us tidings of comfort and joy. It is the Christmas message carried over into everyday life. Immanuel is not just for the last week in December. He is for every day, world without end.

O come to us, abide with us, our Lord Immanuel.

(Hymns: O come, O come, Emmanuel!; O little town of Bethlehem.)

5. RELAXATION

Isaiah 30.15 *'Thus said the Lord God, the Holy One of Israel: In returning and rest you shall be saved; in quietness and trust shall be your strength.'*

Aim: To teach the importance of physical relaxation as a means to a quiet and restful spirit.

As soon as it was discovered that my wife and I were about to become proud parents, a health visitor called to invite my wife to the local antenatal clinic to attend relaxation classes. So, during the long weeks of waiting, every Tuesday afternoon would see her learning and practising the art of relaxation to the accompaniment of piped music and the intoned instructions of the lady in charge. I used to wonder why they didn't think that the father was in need of it as well.

It was, of course, very valuable, and when the time came for the birth my wife's ability to relax her muscles and not to be tense made for a relatively painless delivery – which was just as well because it turned out to be twins she was carrying.

When I read the Old Testament I wonder why the Church does not herself organize relaxation classes for all her members because resting and a cultivated tranquillity are the requirements of the people of God. The Psalmist says it all, in the words immortalized by Kathleen Ferrier in Mendelssohn's famous aria, 'O rest in the Lord, wait patiently for him' (Psalm 37.7). The Lord is frequently described as giving his people rest from all their troubles. And when Jesus extended his great invitation to mankind it was in the terms 'Come unto me, all who are weary and heavy laden, and I will give you rest' (Matthew 11.28).

In a word, the Christian is expected to be a restful person. Relaxing and trusting, waiting patiently and being still – all these are a part of the Bible's vocabulary of faith. The believer is not to be an anxious, strung-up, teeth-gritting model of determination, but a relaxed person, free of cares (because he has cast them on the Lord), no longer burdened by his sins (because they are forgiven through Christ), not fearful of the future (because it is in God's hands). He can relax and rejoice, because he trusts; he has learnt to lean upon his God.

So Isaiah can say, 'He who believes will not be in haste' (28.16). There is no need for panic, no unseemly rush, God can be trusted and his timetable is always right. This shows the importance for the Christian of a faith that relaxes, and it is relaxation that our text is all about. There are three points that I think we should note.

1. *The bond between the physical and the spiritual*

We think of relaxation as a purely physical matter and faith as a purely spiritual attitude, but there is a much closer connection between the two. I believe that we can actually grow in faith as we learn to relax our bodies. We must not separate them from each other. A taut body makes for an anxious soul.

So, practise the art of relaxation. Try it out every morning as you begin your prayers. Talk to your body and tell it to relax – begin with the muscles of the neck, then the arms, then the trunk and finally the legs. Let all your muscles consciously slacken, and when you are relaxed, begin to pray:

'Jesus I am resting, resting in the joy of what thou art,
I am finding out the greatness of thy loving heart.'

You will finish your prayers better able to face the world and the demands of another day. Your body and your spirit alike are at one with God.

When this art is once learnt it can be put to frequent use; in the train, at a conference, at your desk, in those few moments after your midday meal. It is just one more way of taking your faith into your daily life.

2. *Relaxation does not mean freedom from conflict*

The Christian is engaged in conflict every minute of the day: life is a constant battle against the powers of darkness. We are not advocating a quietism that avoids the real issues and problems of life. We were not told to take the whole armour of God so that we might sleep more soundly inside it! Conflict there certainly will be. But there is a better chance of victory if we go into battle relaxed than if we are all keyed up.

Watch an athlete as he approaches the starting-blocks for a race. He is for ever shaking the muscles in his arms and calf and thigh. They must not be allowed to bind; they must be slack and relaxed, so that as the gun goes his body can leap into action and achieve its peak of ability.

So too, the Christian must be at ease if he is to run well. There is really no limit to what he can cope with if he comes to it with a light, free heart. But let him give way to tension, and the demands of life seem to get progressively worse until he is dangerously near to breaking-point.

Now, I am not saying that a nervous breakdown is due to lack of faith. That would be too unfeeling and a gross over-simplification. All kinds of factors combine to bring us to breaking-point, many of them being factors over which we have no control at all. But I do say that if we believe in God and cultivate this relaxed faith as part of our spiritual routine, we shall be able to face the pressures of living with much greater calm and resilience, and that is what we must patiently learn to do.

3. *There is no trust without turning*

'In returning and rest you shall be saved.' The prophets were quick to stress that no man could turn to God except by turning away from his evil ways – from anything, in fact, which kept him from the Lord. This repentance is the prerequisite for faith.

Jeremiah said so: 'If you return, I will restore you, and you shall stand before me' (15.19). For Ezekiel, repentance was a key word: 'If a wicked man turns away from all his sins which he has committed . . . he shall surely live; he shall not die' (18.21). Amos pleaded for the people to return to the Lord: 'I gave you cleanness of teeth in all your cities, and lack of bread in all your places, yet you did not return to me, says the Lord' (4.6). The Psalmist sees that repentance and faith are both due to the initiative of God, when he writes:

'Turn again, O God of hosts! Look down from heaven and see. . .

Then we will never turn back from thee; give us life, and we will call on thy name!

Restore us, O Lord God of hosts! Let thy face shine, that we may be saved!' (Psalm 80.14–19).

Yes, it is God who gives us the ability to jettison our wrong attitudes, to change our direction, to give up past habits, to let go of ourselves and our sins and to relax before him in a trustful, restful faith. We cannot do it ourselves: it is a gift from God. And it is a gift worth having and well worth cultivating.

Prayer: Give us, Lord, the rest of faith, that we may trust you with all our heart, with all our soul, with all our mind and with all our strength; and may find in you our peace and our serenity.

(*Hymns*: *My faith looks up to thee; O for a closer walk with God; Have faith in God, my heart; Lord of all hopefulness, Lord of all joy.*)

6. NEW STRENGTH

Isaiah 40.31 *'But they who wait for the Lord shall renew their strength, they shall mount up with wings like eagles, they shall run and not be weary, they shall walk and not faint.'*

Aim: To teach the spiritual resources which are available to God's servants. The sermon is suitable for many occasions but particularly for services of commissioning.

Here is one of the nuggets of the Old Testament. Its origin is a matter of complete indifference to us, because we know as we read it that it speaks to us in our present condition. It is a word for the timid, for the jaded, for the under-confident and for the over-tired. At some stage or other every one of us needs what this verse says.

1. *The primacy of prayer*

Serving Jesus Christ is a very demanding occupation. As a young choirboy I used to be very amused by the hymn which began 'Ye servants of the Lord, each in his office wait'. Somehow I knew it was not like that at all. But the phrase 'waiting upon the Lord' is open to similar misunderstanding. This verse teaches that Christian service involves running (busy activity), walking (steady routine) and waiting (quiet contemplation), and of these it is the last which releases the strength for doing the other two. So, however busily engaged we may be in doing God's work, we must never neglect the time for reflection, the place of prayer, the importance of being close with God. Retreat prepares the way for advance.

2. *The promise of power*

In a memorable passage the Preacher wrote: 'Again I saw that under the sun the race is not to the swift, nor the battle to the strong, nor bread to the wise, nor riches to the intelligent, nor favour to the men of skill' (Eccles. 9.11). What he was trying to say was that human energy and resources alone are not sufficient to guarantee success and achievement. This is certainly true in God's service. Often it is only when we come to the end of our own resorces that we find God's strength made perfect in our weakness.

The prophet speaks about *renewing* strength, and this conjures up a picture of flagging energies being restored, but that is not strictly the case. A look at the meaning of the Hebrew word translated 'renew' suggests other pictures.

Take, for instance, the passing in Job 14.7. 'There is hope for a tree, if it be cut down, that it will sprout again, and that its shoots will not cease. Though its root grow old in the earth, and its stump die in the ground, yet at the scent of water it will bud and put forth branches like a young plant.' Now the interesting thing to note is that the word translated 'sprout again' in Job is the very word translated 'renew' in Isaiah 40.

So the picture changes to that of a strong Christian leader, always busy, striving for success, a tower of strength in the eyes of his fellow men, suddenly felled by failure or ill health or breakdown and cut down to size. And to him the promise comes that as he waits upon the Lord in his new-found weakness, strength will sprout again like the shoots from a fallen tree.

Another word-picture is to be found in Genesis 35.2. Jacob says to his household, 'Put away the foreign gods that are among you, and purify yourselves, and change your garments; then let us arise and go up to Bethel. . . .' This time the Hebrew word for 'to renew' (strength) is found in the phrase '*change* your garments'. The renewal of strength is like a change of clothing.

It needs little imagination to go on from there to see that as we wait upon God he supplies us with a fresh set of clothes for every new situation he puts us into. As new demands are put upon us, so God's wardrobe provides an ever-changing supply of clothing tailored perfectly to meet our needs.

We have grown accustomed to think of being clothed in the robe of Christ's righteousness or of being invested with the whole armour of God, but this picture takes the metaphor further still. Such is the promise of God's ever-changing but ever-ready power for those who wait upon him.

3. *The grace of perspective*

The eagle is frequently used in Scripture as a symbol of power, though never of brute strength. For that a lion or an ox would be more appropriate. The eagle's greatness lies in its ability to rise above the trivia of life on earth and to soar heavenwards on its mighty wings. Then from its exalted height it can look down upon the world and see life from a different perspective.

It is this 'grace of perspective' which is hinted at by the prophet in our text. It is essential to the Christian worker to be able to see his work from afar, to get away from its day-to-day involvement and to view it objectively, critically, strategically. The eagle's-eye view is a perspective we need consciously to cultivate.

4. *The gift of perseverance*

There is a great deal of routine in every job, and the Christian ministry is no exception. In his Second Letter to the Corinthians Paul lists all the sufferings he has borne for the sake of God's people – floggings, imprisonment, shipwreck and other dangers – but at the end of the paragraph he adds 'And apart from other things there is the daily pressure upon me of my anxiety for all the churches' (2 Cor. 11.28). This is the constant toll that drains the energies of the man of God, and that is often a more likely cause of breakdown than the major catastrophe that breaks over his head. Like a mother's responsibility for her children, it is there all the time. There is no let-up.

But for those who give primacy to prayer there is the assurance given that in the routine walk as well as in the runs of activity, God supplies the gift of perseverance, the ability not to faint or, as Paul put it in another place, 'not grow weary in well-doing' (Gal. 6.9). Tired we certainly shall be. Exhausted we need never be. God's resources are inexhaustible.

Prayer: O Lord Jesus Christ, when you were on earth you were always about your father's business. Grant that we may not grow weary in well-doing. Give us grace to do all in your name. Be to us the pattern whom we follow, the redeemer in whom we trust, the master whom we serve, the friend to whom we look. May we never shrink from our duty from any fear of man. Make us faithful unto death; and bring us at last into your eternal presence, where with the Father and the Holy Spirit you live and reign for ever. (**after** E. B. Pusey)

(*Hymns: Father hear the prayer we offer; Awake, our souls! Away our fears; Give us the wings of faith to rise; Jesus, where'er thy people meet.*)

7. 'PREPARE THE WAY OF THE LORD'

Isaiah 40.3 '*A voice cries: "In the wilderness prepare the way of the Lord, make straight in the desert a highway for our God".*'

Aim: To help people to identify themselves with the mission of John the Baptist in preparing the way for Christ's coming. This would also be suitable for the Nativity of John the Baptist (June 24) or for the third Sunday in Advent.

This is the text on which John the Baptist based his description of himself when he was being questioned by a delegation of priests and Levites from Jerusalem. 'Who are you?' they said. 'Let us have an answer for those who sent us. What do you say about yourself?' He said, 'I am the voice of one crying in the wilderness. Make straight the way of the Lord, as the prophet Isaiah said' (John 1.22,23).

It was a modest reply and it contrasts strangely with our Lord's assessment of him in Matthew 11.11: 'Truly, I say to you, among those born of women there has risen no one greater than John the Baptist.' Which is a remarkable testimony to his importance, even though Jesus did follow it up with the enigmatic words, 'Yet he who is least in the kingdom of heaven is greater than he'.

John the Baptist is surrounded by such mystery statements. He is an endless subject for sermons. Today I want to look more closely at this Isaiah text which served as the mirror in which John saw himself reflected.

Isaiah chapter 40 takes the reader into a different world from the Jerusalem of Ahaz and Hezekiah, Isaiah and the Assyrian invasion, which was the setting for chapters 1 to 39. A century and a half rolls by without so much as a mention and we are launched into the trauma of the Babylonian exile. Half the population of Jerusalem is in captivity seven hundred miles away from home and has been there for anything up to forty years already. A generation has died and is being replaced. If it were not for that incredible nationalism which has always marked the children of Abraham, they would long since have lost their identity. But they live on in exile, proud to be Jews, committed to the Jerusalem that many of them have never seen, wondering when they will return and praying that it may be soon.

To these people the prophet brings a message untypical of Old Testament prophecy. A message of comfort and not of judgement. The days of Israel's sufferings are numbered. Her warfare is ended, her iniquity is pardoned; she has received double punishment for all her sins. Soon it will be over.

Then comes our text, followed by the cry: 'The glory of the Lord shall be revealed, and all flesh shall see it together, for the mouth of the Lord has spoken.'

It is, of course, poetry of quite outstanding beauty and majesty, and only the Authorised Version really conveys the splendour of the original, even if it is at the expense of some technical accuracy. We can be grateful that, if the AV ever falls into total disuse, its wording will be retained for ever in Handel's 'Messiah'. So what does it mean?

The prophet's gospel is that the Lord is coming to rescue his people. We cannot be sure if he means that the Lord is making the journey across the desert to rescue the exiles or that he is bringing the exiles with him across the desert and home to Jerusalem. Poetry is rarely so specific. In any case the language is symbolic and not literal. Its meaning extends more widely than over one particular incident of national deliverance. Take for instance –

1. *The wilderness*

The people of the Old Testament never lived more than a few miles from the wilderness. It extended beyond the boundaries of the fields surrounding every town or village. Everywhere it encroached. It was a continual struggle to keep it at bay. It could be unfriendly but it could also be a place of discipline and testing. Many of the great characters in the Bible did a spell of training in the desert: Moses, David, Paul, and of course John the Baptist himself. Israel's forty years in the wilderness were a punishment for their sins, though they could have been a means of grace. It all depended on how you viewed it.

At its simplest the wilderness was where God was not: the barren, intractable land which was cursed by the Fall. But that did not mean that God could not be found there. In fact, he specialized in transforming deserts, so that they blossomed like the rose or were turned into pools of standing water.

The exile was more than a symbolic wilderness experience for Israel. It was literally so. For thousands of city-dwellers to be taken from Jerusalem and dumped in the desert was enough to make anyone feel God-forsaken. But God was coming to them in the wilderness – just as centuries later he was to come in the person of Jesus Christ to the spiritual wastes of first century Palestine; and as he comes to our barren emptiness and transforms it into life and beauty.

2. *The highway*

Preparing a highway in the desert for God's arrival is a graphic metaphor. It suggests that although God's salvation is his own sovereign act, to which we can contribute nothing, nevertheless there is a part which we can play in preparing the ground. Removing unnecessary obstructions, filling in potholes, levelling the way, so that his coming is made easier. The prophet called upon the exiles to prepare their hearts for the coming of the Lord. John the Baptist saw his mission as preparing the hearts of others so that they would receive him willingly. The Christian is still called upon to prepare the ground for Christ to come to the hearts and lives of the men and women whom he has redeemed.

Removing stones and shovelling earth is a back-breaking job. It has to be done by hand and at close quarters, not by massive bulldozers operated by remote control. The forerunner's task is lowly and tiring, but it must be done. An army of John the Baptists is still needed if Christ is going to show us the glory of the Lord in the salvation of the world. The way has to be prepared – by us.

3. *The voice*

Our text speaks of a voice but of no speaker. Was it his own voice, God's voice or another man's? We cannot tell. It was anonymous. Only the message was important.

John the Baptist wanted his name to go down in history as the man who didn't count. He was merely the forerunner, a human signpost, to point to Jesus and to draw all men's attention to him. 'He must increase, but I must decrease' was how he put it. 'He who is coming after me is mightier than I, whose sandals I am not worthy to carry' (Matthew 3.11)

Only a man of real stature can talk like that. Lesser mortals spend their lives asserting themselves, asking for more, seeking recognition, striving to be noticed. John the Baptist was happy to be forgotten, provided that he was heard. His was the quality of meekness which the New Testament prized so highly – of greatness wearing the clothing of a servant, of leadership girding itself with a towel.

These three images are symbols of John the Baptist's ministry, as they should be of ours as well. The wilderness which hems us in on every side; the highway which we are daily working to prepare for the time when Christ will come; and the voice, both his and ours, which speaks of Jesus and points to him.

Prayer: Give us, O God, something of the spirit of your servant, John the Baptist: his moral courage, his contentment with

simplicity, his faithfulness in witnessing to Christ. So
may we be heralds of Christ and of his kingdom, and
make ready his way, to the glory of his name.

(*Hymns: On Jordan's bank the Baptist's cry; Sing we the praises of the
great forerunner; Lo, in the wilderness a voice.*)

8. 'I AM DOING A NEW THING'

Isaiah 43. 18,19 *'Remember not the former things, nor consider the
things of old. Behold, I am doing a new thing; now it springs
forth, do you not perceive it?'*

Aim: To encourage people to look forwards rather than back-
wards and to look for signs of God's activity in their midst. This
would be suitable for use on an anniversary, patronal festival or
feast of dedication, or at the beginning of a New Year.

An anniversary can be an opportunity for unrestrained nostalgia
– and why not? Every time the second Saturday in August
comes round, my wife and I remember the same day years ago
when it rained and rained but nothing dampened the delight of
our wedding day. We look back at the black-and-white photo-
graphs of guests reflected in puddles and we laughingly relive
the details we can remember – the friends who came, the singing
of the college choir, the reception (somewhat blurred), the taxi-
chase to the station.

A church too has its memories: former clergy, days of prayer,
the verger who kept a goat in the churchyard, the broadcast
service. And today we are entitled to look back – with a smile or
a sigh – to days that are past. That's what anniversaries are for.

But my text appears to rebuke us. 'Remember not the former
things, nor consider the things of old.' I don't think this is
because it is wrong to look back, and the last thing I want to do
on a special occasion is to strike a discordant note. It is rather

because too much looking back can blind us to what God is doing today. Something different, something new.

It is a healthy thing for a parish from time to time to sit back and look at itself and assess its progress. What has it achieved? Where are its chief weaknesses? What are its immediate objectives? How can they be attained? Sometimes a parish asks an outsider – the rural dean or the archdeacon – to come in and act as a consultant while they go through the exercise. It is never time wasted. But there is one question that is often missed out from such an enquiry: 'What is *God* doing in the parish?'

The key to successful parochial ministry is not to be found simply in good planning, strategic use of resources and enthusiastic leadership. It has to do with observing the activity of God; listening for the signs of the Spirit's moving and then, to change the metaphor, setting your sails to catch that wind of God wherever it wafts or gusts through the parish.

God works in many different ways, and in the book of Isaiah the prophet uses a number of examples to illustrate the new thing that he is on the point of doing.

1. *Restoration*

Notice how verse 19 goes on: 'I will make a way in the wilderness and rivers in the desert.' Before we rush into allegory, remember that when the prophet first spoke these words he was intending a *literal* fulfilment. God was going to transform the vast tract of desert that effectively separated Jerusalem and Judah from Babylon and the Hebrew exiles. Instead of it being an impenetrable barrier it was going to become a corridor along which the exiles could return to their homes in safety. It would still be arid, sun-baked desert, but there would be a pathway to follow and sufficient water to drink. In a word, the prisoners could come home.

We cannot apply this text to the repatriation of refugees today, though many may find hope and the possibility of returning to the land of their birth in a passage like this. The prophet is not offering every generation of displaced persons the promise of getting back to where they once belonged. That would be altogether too naive. For the Judean exile Jerusalem was more than home, it was God and worship and temple. Separated from it he felt spiritually bereft. So the exile was a spiritual problem of the greatest magnitude.

The Old Testament prophets offered two answers. One was that God would go and join his people in exile – this was part at any rate of the significance of Ezekiel's vision of God by the banks of the river Chebar – and the other was that God would bring them home. Isaiah stressed this second path. Lost and derelict as they were, the exiled people would find a way back to Jerusalem and to God, despite the apparent impossibility of it all.

With this we must surely equate God's 'new thing' in the gospel of our Lord Jesus Christ. Whether we express this in the children's chorus 'There's a way back to God from the dark paths of sin' or use more sophisticated language, we know that through Christ the new and living way to God has been opened up and through him lost people can find their way back home. This is God's good news which never grows old. Our Church was founded upon it, and on this anniversary God is reminding us of that fact and saying to us: 'This is the new thing that I am doing – do you not perceive it?'

2. *Cleansing*

Look now at verse 25: 'I, I am He who blots out your transgressions for my own sake, and I will not remember your sins.' It is a verse which brings us face to face with the age-old problem of guilt. Although much is said about it today, as the root cause of so much insecurity, neurosis and disease, it was just as great a problem, I am sure, in biblical times.

The evidence of the state of Hebrew religion at the time of the exile shows that the sense of ritual defilement incurred by long years in a heathen land was a very serious problem which the prophets had to deal with. There was the conflict over who was fit to rebuild the temple. Should the returned exiles do it, or were they too contaminated by life in Babylon? Should the 'people of the land' do it, who had stayed in Judea all through the Babylonian occupation, or were they equally defiled by compromise and by their acquiescence in the burned-out ruins of God's temple? Beneath the charges and countercharges lay the submerged feelings of guilt and unworthiness. The more men protest the more they betray their own vulnerability.

Behind today's strident, belligerent voices lies a similar sense of guilt. The economic guilt of our failure to cope with the variations of wealth and poverty. The domestic guilt over responsibility for ageing relatives ('was I right to put mother in a home?') or the parent's worry over wayward teenagers ('what did we do wrong?') or the unmarried mother living with the memory of her panic decision to dispose of her unwanted foetus. The guilt that is felt by the person in senior management who knows that the decisions he makes can blight the lives of hundreds of workers and their families. Small wonder that the world is overloaded with people who cannot look themselves in the eye or who suffer from the after-effects of stifled consciences. They cannot forgive themselves because they have no God to assure them that they can be forgiven.

To all such people God offers full and complete forgiveness through Christ. The prophets did not argue the point, they simply proclaimed it. God is a forgiving God, an accepting God – for all those who will turn to him. The disqualifying factors are stubbornness ('hardness of heart'), refusal to repent, continuing disobedience to God's known will, secret idolatry. Forgiveness is free, but it is not cheap. Many will baulk at the cost. But for those who turn to God, cleansing from sin and guilt is guaranteed.

This is the Church's ministry of absolution. Perhaps it should not be called a 'new thing', but it is certainly a very 'renewing thing' for the one who experiences it. 'Do you not perceive it?' says the prophet.

3. Renewal

The prophet goes on: 'I will pour my Spirit upon your descendants, and my blessing on your offspring. They shall spring up like grass amid waters, like willows by flowing streams' (44.3,4) These words speak of the luxuriant growth that comes with new life. The Spirit is nearly always described in the Bible as being given 'to you (the present generation) and to your descendants (the younger generation)'. God is for ever looking forwards to the future and it is in the future that his richest blessings are to be found, not in the past.

What can we reasonably expect God's Spirit to do in this parish during the coming year? If there is dry land, where nothing seems to grow or flourish – an unresponsive youth group, a moribund women's meeting, a block of flats where there is no Christian witness – look to the Spirit to perform a life-giving miracle there. Everywhere look for signs of life and new growth. Expect new Christians to emerge in unexpected quarters, as in verse 5 – 'This one will say, "I am the Lord's", another will call himself by the name of Jacob, and another will write on his hand, "The Lord's".' So whether it comes about through a rash of 'Jesus stickers' or by people quietly identifying themselves as being on the Lord's side, we can and should be watchful for the Spirit to be at work in our midst.

It begins by our believing that God will act. This is why he says 'Behold I am doing a new thing: now it springs forth, *do you not perceive it?*'

Prayer: Give us, Lord, the eyes to see what you are about to do in this your church and in this your parish. Keep us on our knees in prayer and on our toes in expectancy. We believe that you are able and we believe that you will, through Jesus Christ our Lord.

(*Hymns*: *Spirit of mercy, truth and love; God is working his purpose out as year succeeds to year; All my hope on God is founded.*)

9. MAN OF SORROWS

Isaiah 53.3 *'He was despised and rejected by men; a man of sorrows, and acquainted with grief; and as one from whom men hide their faces he was despised, and we esteemed him not.'*

Aim: To provide a meditation on the Cross, built around the Suffering Servant of Isaiah 53 and suitable for use on Good Friday or in Holy Week.

It is never easy to understand what is going on in another person's mind, and yet the more you love someone, the more you want to know. 'What are you thinking about?' must be the question most commonly asked by young lovers of each other.

When we come to Holy Week and to the sufferings and death of Christ, we try to get close to him and to understand what he was feeling and thinking during the closing moments of his life on earth. If we are to believe St. Luke, he was thinking about Isaiah chapter 53. Luke 22.37 quotes Jesus as saying: 'I tell you that this scripture must be fulfilled in me, "And he was reckoned with transgressors".' The reference is to Isaiah 53.12. He goes on: 'For *what is written about me* has its fulfilment'. This is the clue to our meditation today: Jesus said about this chapter in Isaiah – 'It is written about me'. If so, he must have used it as the model for his sufferings and sacrificial death. Let us, therefore, look at the Cross and at the one who hung and suffered there and be helped in doing so by these memorable words.

I want to speak about our crucified Saviour with the help of four headings: his sorrows – the kind of man he was; his stripes – what he actually endured; his silence – how he bore it all; and his sinbearing – what it signified eternally.

1. *His sorrows*

He was a man of sorrows and acquainted with grief, and here is the first big question-mark over him. So much so that the prophet begins the chapter with words of astonishment, 'Who has believed what we have heard? To whom has the arm of the Lord been revealed?' The answer to the first question is that no one will believe this, and the answer to the second question is that the Lord has revealed his arm – to a weakling! A young plant! A root out of dry ground! Not a handsome, ruddy-faced hero like David, but a pathetic figure with no natural beauty or human attractiveness. A man despised and rejected by a world that esteems only success and stardom.

God has a way of turning human values upside down. Who would expect a man of sorrows to save the world? Who would expect weakness to triumph over the powers of darkness? God appears to do things that way round in order to remind us that his ways are not our ways and his thoughts are not our thoughts. He has chosen the weak things of the world to confound the things which are mighty. And in so doing he has shown that sufferings and pain are not evils but can be redemptive.

The problem of suffering is not exclusive to the twentieth century. For hundreds of years before Christ it occupied the minds of thinkers and writers, and the Old Testament bears witness to how the Hebrews wrestled with it. Someone has said that there are three distinct levels of understanding to be found in the Old Testament writings. The first is that *all sufferers are sinners*. This is the view expressed by Job's comforters and its fallacy is there for all to see. Nevertheless it persisted and is sometimes heard even today, especially in the form of the question, 'What have I done to deserve it?'

The second level is reached through the experiences of men like Jeremiah who suffered but did not waver in their faith. It is that *some sufferers are saints*, and they would not be saints unless they had the opportunity to learn through suffering. The third and highest level is that of Isaiah 53, namely, that *some sufferers are saviours*, and this comes out supremely in the Christ of whom the chapter speaks. To be the Saviour of the world he must first have been the man of sorrows.

2. *His stripes*

Good Friday is the day when we spend much time thinking about the sufferings Christ bore for us: the mocking, the scourging, the crown of thorns, and eventually the nails of the cross. Many Christians like to spend the three hours from noon until mid-afternoon in prayer and meditation, reliving the scene and trying to learn from it. It can be a most rewarding experience.

The important thing to remember is that it was all *for you*. That's what makes it so personal. I sit and listen to the gruesome details of the passion story and I say to myself: 'He did it for me – how greatly Jesus must have loved me!' And you can say the same. 'With his stripes we are healed.'

3. *His silence*

In an English court of law it is often assumed that a defendant who refuses to go into the dock to defend himself has something to hide. And we are used to the spectacle of terrorist prisoners contemptuously ignoring everything that is said to them because they say they do not recognize the authority of the court. Jesus' silence was of a very different kind. It was the silence of innocent suffering when faced with evil men determined to have their way. It was the silence of total submission to the good will of God even when it was being achieved by the ill will of twisted men. 'Like a lamb that is led to the slaughter, and like a sheep that before its shearers is dumb, so he opened not his mouth' (53.7).

The picture of the sheep links the Redeemer with the redeemed. We are like sheep who have gone astray. He is like the sheep that is sacrificed for our sins. But instead of being an unblemished animal waiting to have its throat cut to atone for someone's sins, the victim is a blameless man waiting to be lifted up on a cross so that he can draw the whole world to himself. He said nothing; no words of accusation, no self-pity, no histrionics. He never said a mumbling word. It is an example to every sufferer – and much more besides.

4. *His sinbearing*

It is not easy to echo the words of verse 10 and to say that it was the will of the Lord to bruise him and that he (the Lord) has put him to grief. What is the Lord doing causing unnecessary suffering – and to his Messiah too? But the following words explain it. 'When he makes himself an offering for sin, he shall . . . prolong his days; the will of the Lord shall prosper in his hand.' The death of Jesus Christ on the cross was none other than the Son of God making himself an offering for sin, the Sinless One dying for the sins of the world. It was what God the Father intended, and what God the Son freely chose to do.

This was the way through to the victory of the cross. Out of spiritual travail would come light and satisfaction. In place of death and oblivion would come a family and the continuing life of his body, the Church. 'He shall see his offspring, he shall prolong his days.' Many will be justified, accounted righteous; the sins of many will be borne. By being numbered with sinners in his dying, Christ can stand between sinners and the due punishment of their sins.

All this is the wonder of Calvary, for which Isaiah 53 prepares the way as it also prepared our Lord for going that way. Never have prediction and fulfilment been more closely matched. Here is the gospel in the Old Testament, good news about a Man of Sorrows.

Prayer: Lord Jesus Christ, as we mediate upon your dying love
on this great day of our redemption, bring it home to us
that you gave yourself for all men and especially that you
gave yourself for us.

(*Hymns*: *Man of sorrows, what a name; When I survey the wondrous
Cross; O crucified Redeemer, whose life-blood we have spilt;
There is a green hill far away*.)

10. THE GREAT INVITATION

Isaiah 55.1 *Ho, every one who thirsts, come to the waters; and he who
has no money, come, buy and eat! Come, buy wine and milk
without money and without price.'*

Aim: To extend the invitation of the gospel, showing that this is
to be found in the pages of the Old Testament as well as of the
New. The whole chapter deserves to be read to the congregation.

Today's visitor to the Holy Land soon gets used to the sight of
the water-seller as he walks the streets of the Old City of
Jerusalem offering his wares. It is an ancient and an honourable
occupation, and we only betray our western prejudices by being
shocked to think of water being offered at a price. In a hot
climate it is a valuable commodity and not easy to come by.

Our text appears to be echoing the cry of the water-sellers of
two and a half thousand years ago. 'Ho, every one who thirsts,
come to the waters.' But the speaker is God, and the goods on
offer are spiritual, not material: mercy and pardon and 'my
steadfast, sure love for David'. What is the prophet talking
about?

The Book of Isaiah has been described as the Gospel according
to the Old Testament; and here is the prophet inviting his read-

ers to respond to the love of God and to come to him for for-giveness and new life. It is the kind of language used by our Lord when he said 'Come to me, all who labour and are heavy laden, and I will give you rest', or again, 'If any one thirst, let him come to me and drink'. There are echoes, too, in the parable of the great supper as the invitations go out to the guests, 'Come; for all is now ready', and they began to make excuses.

1. *Excuses*

Isaiah was prepared to be offered excuses instead of acceptances, so he tried to anticipate them. They are the excuses that men and women are still putting up to God to avoid responding to his call. The first is: 'I can't afford it'. The reply comes back: God's mercies are offered freely to all who will come to him. 'Come, buy wine and milk without money and without price.'

By definition, grace is something that neither money nor merit can buy. Yet human nature finds it hard to accept free grace and wants to offer a contribution of some kind towards it. No one likes to feel permanently indebted, not even to God. So we weigh up what we think we can afford and we try to strike a bargain with him. How stupid! Can love be purchased? Can forgiveness be put out to tender? No, it must be free if it is to be the real thing, and we must come to receive it with empty hands.

Consider the 'commodities' that are on offer. Water, wine, milk and bread. These are the easterner's staple resources, the very symbols of life itself. We must not get lost in allegory, but three of them at any rate have sacramental meaning – water, bread and wine – and both milk and bread are symbolic of the word of God in Holy Scripture. The gospel fare of word and sacrament is as freely available to those who come to God today as their counterparts were in Old Testament times.

The second excuse is that this is not for the common man, but only for the privileged few. A religion of high standards and a built-in doctrine of election will inevitably provoke this com-ment. Isaiah met it with an emphatic 'you' (plural), addressed to all Israel, whether exiles or not. 'I will make with *you* an everlast-ing covenant', and he adds, 'my steadfast, sure love for David'. What this means is that God's promises made to one man, David, and his royal successors after him are now being made freely available to all the people of Israel, both high and low.

Privilege has now been extended to the whole people of God. All are members of the royal family!

In much the same way the New Testament Church taught that the gospel was for gentiles as well as Jews. On the day of Pentecost Peter said 'The promise is to you and to your children and to all that are far off, every one whom the Lord our God calls to him' (Acts 2.39). A few chapters later he is found saying to gentile enquirers, 'Truly I perceive that God shows no partiality. . . All the prophets bear witness that every one who believes in him receives forgiveness of sins through his name' (Acts 10.34, 43). The gospel has no exclusive classes. Whosoever will may come. It is only sin that keeps people away and prevents us from coming to the Cross, where all are of equal worth and equally welcome.

Thirdly, there is the excuse of God's remoteness. Now, God *is* remote and infinite and beyond human comprehension, and it is a very human reaction when faced with his call or his claims upon our lives to withdraw into our shell and say lamely, 'It's all above my head'. Isaiah will not have it. The Lord is *not* far away, he is near. 'Seek the Lord while he may be found, call upon him while he is near; let the wicked forsake his way, and the unrighteous man his thoughts; let him return to the Lord, that he may have mercy on him, and to our God, for he will abundantly pardon' (Isa. 55.6f.).

Finally, there is the age-old excuse of 'Some other time'. It was the excuse of Felix before Paul: 'Go away for the present; when I have an opportunity I will summon you' (Acts 24.25). It is the decision of indecision; the 'not now' of those good intentions that pave the way to Hell. The prophet faces up to it squarely, but instead of threatening he pleads and urges. Note the string of imperatives in verses 1–7: come, buy, eat; hearken, eat, delight yourselves; incline your ear, come, hear; seek, call, forsake, return. The evangelist can do no more to spur his hearers into immediate action. All he can do is to press for a decision, and he must do that with every last drop of urgency and sincerity he can muster. The hearer has the right either to decide or to defer – and he must bear the consequences of what he does.

2. *The Power of the Word*

Effective evangelism consists of at least three main ingredients:

(a) presenting the invitation, (b) anticipating the objections, and (c) relying on the work of God's Spirit. We have noticed how Isaiah 55 deals with the first two of these, but what of the third? In these verses the prophet speaks not so much of God's Spirit as of God's Spirit-inspired word. 'For as the rain and the snow come down from heaven, and return not thither but water the earth, making it bring forth and sprout, giving seed to the sower and bread to the eater, so shall my word be that goes forth from my mouth; it shall not return to me empty, but it shall accomplish that which I purpose, and prosper in the thing for which I sent it' (Isa. 55.10f.).

There is an inbuilt power within the prophet's preaching which has a continuing life and influence on those who hear it. The word is spoken, but it doesn't end there. The Spirit drives it along and propels it on its way until it has done its intended work in the lives of men. This belief in the power of the word of God is of immense comfort to the preacher of the gospel. He himself has a heavy responsibility, he knows, but the effective power to convert is God's and not his. One man sows, another man waters, but it is always God who gives the increase.

Here then is Isaiah's great invitation. It comes to us with compelling urgency to accept God's offer of a lifetime. It sweeps away our objections. It presses us to respond without delay. It points us to God's immeasurable love and it tells us that whether we are thirsty for his grace or strangers to his covenant or too poor to purchase our own salvation, we have only to return to the Lord and he will abundantly pardon us. We shall be ransomed, healed, restored, forgiven, through Jesus Christ our Redeemer and our Lord.

Prayer: Let your word, O Lord, do its work within our hearts, drawing us to yourself, leading us to repentance and faith, giving us new life and usefulness in your service.

(*Hymns*: *I heard the voice of Jesus say; Just as I am, without one plea; As pants the hart for cooling streams*.)

11.   A KIND OF FASTING

Isaiah 58. 6–8 *'Is not this the fast that I choose: to loose the bonds of wickedness, to undo the thongs of the yoke, to let the oppressed go free, and to break every yoke? Is it not to share your bread with the hungry, and bring the homeless poor into your house; when you see the naked, to cover him, and not to hide yourself from your own flesh? Then shall your light break forth like the dawn, and your healing shall spring up speedily; your righteousness shall go before you, and the glory of the Lord shall be your rear guard.'*

Aim: To teach the meaning of fasting in terms of human compassion. Isaiah 58 is read on Ash Wednesday (ASB) and this sermon would be suitable for Lent or for any penitential season.

In the Sermon on the Mount, our Lord began one of his sayings with the words *'When you fast*, do not look dismal, like the hypocrites, for they disfigure their faces that their fasting may be seen by men'. Ever since then, Christians have wondered whether and when and how they should fast. Is it really necessary, or beneficial, or a proper thing for post-Reformation Christians to do?

Most of us would answer the last question by quoting Jesus' words again: *'When* you fast', implying that fasting is assumed to be as normal a Christian exercise as praying and giving alms and the other things he spoke about in St Matthew chapters 5–7. The important thing is not *whether* we do it, but *how* we do it.

What kind of fasting shall we be doing this Lent? There is much more to it than a rather facile giving up of cigarettes or chocolate, and Scripture has given us a good deal of helpful teaching on the subject. Let me summarize.

1.   *What fasting is*

(a) Fasting nearly always accompanies prayer. It is an aid to concentration, a mark of our seriousness of purpose. It can even be an incidental consequence of giving ourselves to prayer: we pray and pray until we go hungry. In this context, fasting is never an end in itself.

(b) Fasting is done unobtrusively, as every spiritual exercise should be. No one else need know about it. It is a private matter between ourselves and God. 'When you fast, anoint your head and wash your face, that your fasting may not be seen by men but by your Father who is in secret' (Matt. 6.17f.).

(c) Fasting can be a reminder to ourselves that we are masters of our appetites and not their slaves. From time to time we need to put this to the test, in case we get too soft and self-indulgent. Only by consciously going without things we like can we prove to ourselves that our bodies are under our control. And when doctors tell us that one of the most serious complaints in the western world is not cancer but obesity, we do well to exercise restraint.

(d) Fasting can be practised for some greater good – to save money for a charitable purpose, to bring a measure of seriousness to an easy-going life, to give more time to God or to the needs of others.

2. What fasting is not

Isaiah 58 makes a swingeing attack on those who fast for the wrong reasons. Look at the negatives it proclaims.

(a) Fasting is not a way of bribing God to pay attention to our needs. Verse 3 condemns those who say 'Why have we fasted, and thou seest it not? Why have we humbled ourselves, and thou takest no knowledge of it?' Fasting is never to be used as a weapon against God, or as a sweetener to make him change his mind. That is a false view of grace.

(b) Fasting should never be accompanied by selfishness or hard-heartedness. 'Behold, in the day of your fast you seek your own pleasure and oppress all your workers' (verse 3). Unless the practice of our faith is linked with a practical outworking of Christian standards of love and considerateness, we have got it all wrong.

(c) Fasting is much more than self-abasement. 'Is such the fast that I choose, a day for a man to humble himself? Is it to bow down his head like a rush, and to spread sackcloth and ashes under him? Will you call this a fast, and a day acceptable to the Lord?' (verse 5). The answer is plainly 'No'. Self-inflicted misery is of no greater value than self-inflicted humility. Neither rings true. Neither is pleasing to God.

3. *What does the Lord require?*

Our text gives us the positive dimension. To deny ourselves is not a matter of giving up this luxury or that bad habit. The most practical way of saying No to ourselves is by saying Yes to our brother in his need. What is wanted from us is our commitment to a lifetime of loving service. So this Lent should be marked by positive work for Christ's kingdom under the headings of helping, sharing and caring.

(a) Helping those who are oppressed. We are inclined to think that oppression happens only to those in South Africa or in Communist lands or in San Salvador, but it can be found much nearer home. It is the oppression suffered by the coloured person who is discriminated against, by the ignorant person who is taken in by a high-pressure salesman, by the old person who has no power to make his voice heard in the town hall or a government department. These people need help. They are the weak and downtrodden of today's society. We must not pass them by on the other side of the road. Do you know anyone that you could be helping in such a way?

(b) Sharing the good things that we have. There is a much greater generosity among the poor than you find among the rich. Perhaps the poor man sees his meagre possessions in better perspective. Fasting means giving – letting the hungry and the homeless in on the security we enjoy. Fasting means hospitality freely given. Fasting means sharing, and that can be incredibly costly. If we are going to fast in this way we must count the cost and weigh up what we can do, but it will not be easy or trouble-free.

(c) Caring for our fellow men . . . 'not to hide yourself from your own flesh'. The reference is not to your kith and kin, but to your fellow human being. It was what the priest and the Levite notoriously failed to do with the wounded traveller on the road to Jericho. When they came across need they hid themselves. Behind a cloak of busyness, or of preoccupation with the Lord's affairs, or of fear, or of indifference. The excuse does not matter. The point is that they hid themselves and were condemned.

The Christian way is to see Christ in our brother, whether he is downtrodden or poor or hungry or in need. Instantly he becomes not a tramp but an apostle, not an object of pity but a person to be respected. The challenge of our Lenten fast is not whether we agree that this is so, but what we are going to do about it. If we decide that our Lenten exercise will be to spend five minutes extra in prayer each day, or attend an extra Communion service mid-week, we *could* be guilty of 'hiding ourselves from our own flesh', ignoring the need of our fellow man beneath a cloak of godliness. We must decide what we are going to do. To fast or not to fast, that is the question.

Prayer: We remember, Lord, all those who are in need of any kind – all prisoners of conscience, the homeless and the handicapped, the oppressed and the powerless, those who are confined to their beds or to their homes, the sick in mind and body. Show us how we can help them and serve Christ in serving them.

(Hymns: When I needed a neighbour, were your there, were you there? We find thee, Lord, in others' need; Father, hear the prayer we offer; Jesus, my Lord, how rich thy grace.)

12.   THE MAKING OF A MAN OF GOD

Jeremiah 1.5 *'Before I formed you in the womb I knew you, and before you were born I consecrated you; I appointed you a prophet to the nations.'*

Aim: To discover through the life of Jeremiah something about the call and the qualifications that make a man of God. Passage for study: Jeremiah chapter 1.

In one sense Jeremiah is unique among the prophets of the Old Testament. He was a man of deep sensitivity, and in his writings he laid bare his soul more than any of the other prophets. Perhaps it had something to do with his unpopularity. His message was not calculated to endear him to his compatriots and he was for ever being persecuted and opposed by them. That is why he has earned the description of 'the weeping prophet'. It may also give a clue to why it was that, whenever Jesus was being quizzed about his identity, there was usually a question 'Are you Jeremiah or one of the prophets?' Could it have been that people saw past our Lord's calm exterior and sensed that underneath there was a heart that felt deeply and suffered more than he showed? A man of sorrows and acquainted with grief? If it was, he was certainly in Jeremiah's line of succession.

At the same time Jeremiah is nearer to us than we imagine. He was human, and his humanity comes across in episode after episode. He was introspective and at times under-confident. He had spells when nothing seemed to go right for him and he wished he had never agreed to become a prophet. Yet it had never been a matter of agreement or choice, because the call had been virtually irresistible. So all sorts of Christians read Jeremiah and see something of themselves in him, though at a very much lower level, of course.

I want to look at the first chapter of his prophecy and see what points of similarity exist between a man of God like Jeremiah and a Christian worker like one of us.

1. *His call*

Most of the Old Testament prophets have a story to tell about their call or their first encounter with God. Moses at the burning bush, Samuel as a child, Isaiah in the temple, Ezekiel on the plains of Babylon. Without some such experience none of them would have dared to prophesy – or, if they had, they would have been condemned as false prophets, who spoke out of their own heads and had no knowledge of the living word of God. The true prophet was by definition a man who had met with God.

The encounter had no stereotype, however. No two prophets shared a similar experience of God. Each was peculiar to that individual. God does not go in for conveyor-belt conversions.

In much the same way, today's man of God begins his ministry with an encounter. It may be a call experience, a conversion experience, a charismatic experience, a healing experience. It may, like Jeremiah, come from a deeply-rooted sense of destiny. Whatever it is, it brings the conviction that 'the Lord has laid his hand on me'. That is the prerequisite for Christian service.

2. *His doubts*

Jeremiah's response to God's call was full of hesitation. 'Ah, Lord God! Behold, I do not know how to speak, for I am only a youth.' But please note that it was a hesitation based on inadequacy, not on unwillingness. That is why he was not rebuked or struck dumb, as happened to the father of John the Baptist when he demurred at the angel's message. God accepts and understands our feelings of incompetence – indeed they are often justified – but he has less sympathy with disobedience or refusal.

I am impressed by the way in which God engages with Jeremiah in the resolution of his problems. He does so in three crisp sentences.

(a) 'Do not say, I am only a youth.' There was common ground here between Jeremiah and God. Both knew how old Jeremiah was and that he *was* young! Jeremiah knew his age and felt shackled by it. God knew Jeremiah's age and he said: 'Don't keep harping on it. Accept the fact that you are young; it's a strength as well as a weakness. But, whatever you do, don't keep on about it or you'll talk yourself into a state of helplessness.'

If you have a handicap or a limitation which makes you hesitate to follow the Lord and to answer his call, lay it at his feet and say, 'Lord, you know all about me and my weaknesses. What do you want me to do?'

(b) 'To all to whom I send you you shall go, and whatever I command you you shall speak.' Here is a clear statement that the servant of God is under his Master's orders. He is not responsible for ordering his own life; he is simply to do what the Lord instructs him to do. Both the location of his ministry and the content of his message are to be given him by God. All he has to do is to obey.

(c) 'Be not afraid of them, for I am with you to deliver you.' Jeremiah was going to have many enemies to face – kings, nobles, prophets, priests, soldiers, Judeans, Babylonians – but in every confrontation God would be with him. The Lord never sends his disciples out alone. He always accompanies them himself. The final words of Jesus come to mind: 'Go therefore and make disciples of all nations, baptizing them in the name of the Father and of the Son and of the Holy Spirit, teaching them to observe all that I have commanded you; and lo, I am with you always, to the close of the age' (Matthew 28.19,20).

3. *His message*

Although God promised to put his words into Jeremiah's mouth, the content of the message was summed up for him in two mini-visions. The first was of an almond branch, the second was of a boiling pot. What do they mean?

(a) The almond branch. I don't suppose there was anything strange or supernatural about this. It had probably been growing outside Jeremiah's kitchen window for years. But suddenly God used it to convey a message. The almond tree was the herald of spring. Its flowers appeared before its leaves, and the first sign of the almond blossom cheered everyone up with the prospect of new life and warmer days ahead. So the almond earned its Hebrew name of 'the waker'.

Now, said God to Jeremiah, if the almond wakes up with messages of spring, can you not think of me too as the wakeful one, watching over my word, bringing signs of hope and life? It was a fairly obvious play on words but it was more than that. God was teaching Jeremiah that he was alive and active and involved. The almond branch was a message of hope: God was not dead.

(b) The boiling pot. The picture here is less clear, but it looks as if the vision referred to a cauldron which was slightly on the tip, so that as the contents bubbled away they boiled over into the fire towards the south. 'Then the Lord said to me, "Out of the north evil shall break forth upon all the inhabitants of the land" ' (verse 14). This has been variously interpreted – of Scythian tribesmen raiding Judah, of the Babylonian armies invading many years later, of the perennial threat that came from the north.

For our purposes, however, the boiling pot is to be taken as a symbol of danger and of God's judgement. Jeremiah needed to learn that his message was not complete without the element of solemn warning. It was his job to teach the people not only that God was beginning to work and to bring life but that he would bring judgement if the people did not take heed to his words and mend their ways.

These two elements should be present in every preacher's ministry even now: the almond branch of hope and life, and the boiling pot of warning and judgement. 'Christ is coming' is one half of our message; 'to judge the world' is the other half.

4.   *His strength*

This chapter concludes with a reassuring promise which was to serve the young prophet for the long years of conflict that lay ahead of him. 'Behold, I make you this day a fortified city, an iron pillar, and bronze walls, against the whole land, against the kings of Judah, its princes, its priests and the people of the land' (verse 18). Young and inexperienced as he was, he was going to be made indestructible and rock like in the face of his critics and his foes.

If we study the life of Jeremiah through the pages of his prophecy, we shall find that to the end of his days he was caught up in the contradiction between his desire to serve his people and his loyalty to the word of God which they refused to heed. So from a human point of view his ministry was a failure. He was never allowed to be encouraged by the sweet taste of success. He needed to be as hard as iron if he was going to be God's man for God's work. But he was given the grace of endurance and he persevered to the end, a living example of strength coming out of weakness.

Prayer: Help us your servants, Lord, to be men of God, Men of courage, men of truth, men of prayer; and keep us humble in your service and confident in your sufficiency, for Jesus Christ's sake.

(Hymns: Fight the good fight with all thy might; Be thou my guardian and my guide; Lord God, thou art our maker and our end.)

13.   **THE TWO TREES**

Jeremiah 17.7 *'Blessed is the man who trusts in the Lord, whose trust is the Lord.'*

Aim: To explain the nature of true religion, which is bound up with the direction of a person's faith, and to lead people into a living faith in God through Christ. Passage to be read: Jeremiah 17. 5–10.

Palestine is a land of remarkable contrasts. It can be very hot and it can be very cold. Compare the stifling heat of Tel Aviv in the *hamsin* (the oppressive desert wind) with Jerusalem on a frosty winter's night. Or consider the variety of vegetation. At one spot there is a superabundance of lush green grass and plant-life. A mile away you can find nothing but barren wilderness where nothing survives but an occasional goat and the ubiquitous lizard.

Among the coloured slides I brought back with me from a year spent in Israel in my student days are two which I have often shown to illustrate this point. One is a close-up of a magnificent red bougainvillea filling the screen with a riot of colour, and guaranteed to arouse the 'oohs' of any audience. The other, slightly over-exposed, is a picture of unrelieved desert sand shimmering with a scorching heat into the dazzled eyes of the viewers. Now, the remarkable thing about these two slides is that both were taken from the exact same spot, one facing one way, one the other. What made all the difference? Irrigation. Water.

1. *Two kinds of faith*

It was the continual sight of contrasts like these that led Jeremiah (and others before him) to the simile of the two trees – the shrub in the desert and the tree planted by water. They were a picture of two kinds of man, the self-reliant and the God-fearer. Psalm 1 uses similar language but there the contrast is between the righteous whose 'delight is in the law of the Lord, and on his law he meditates day and night' and the wicked who is 'like chaff which the wind drives away'.

Jeremiah's contrasting pair are not judged by their morality – good or bad – but by their *faith*. 'Cursed is the man who trusts in man' and 'blessed is the man who trusts in the Lord'. Both men have faith, but it is only faith in the Lord which brings salvation and blessing. Faith by itself is merely an attitude, a direction in which one looks for strength and help. It is not the faith that saves, it is the one in whom the faith is placed. Let us look at these two types more closely.

2. *The shrub in the desert*

First comes the picture of self-reliance, the shrub in the desert. The tree referred to is the dwarf juniper, commonly found in rocky cliffs and barren places of the desert. It is an interesting word because it is associated with a Hebrew root meaning 'stripped' or 'naked', the idea being that this particular shrub looks bare and unadorned. So, like the barren fig-tree which Jesus cursed, the man who clothes himself with self-confidence will find it being stripped off him and he withers away to a mere shadow of his former glory.

The reason for this decline is quite simple. The roots do not penetrate down to the water-level beneath the surface of the desert. So, even if improvement comes, the tree derives no benefit. 'Because it had no depth of earth it withered away', said Jesus about the seed scattered on the shallow soil. Self-confidence is a shallow foundation on which to build a character. It cannot survive the tests of scorching heat and minimal rainfall.

We can take this analogy a stage further. The temptations we find hardest to face are the spiritual droughts of discouragement and loneliness. They strip us of our buoyancy and leave us parched and dry. It is only the tap-root of faith in God's all-sufficiency that keeps us from withering away totally. The man who professes to be self-sufficient finds he has nothing more to draw upon and he succumbs. He is like the shrub in the desert.

3. *The tree by the water*

The other tree could not be more different. The tree by the water has a better situation ('by the stream'), a deeper root-system, more luxuriant foliage, and a healthy crop of fruit. This is the picture of the man who trusts in the Lord. He draws on the unseen waters of God's Spirit and his life shows what a difference this can make.

Note that in one respect at any rate the two trees share the same environment. They both face the year of drought, the time when the heat comes. The Christian must not expect to avoid the searing heat of persecution or the barren wastes of spiritual dryness. But, unlike the self-reliant man, he is not afraid of them, and the more he experiences hard times the more confident he is in the supply of God's unseen resources to keep him fresh and fruitful.

It is in fact only in the times of drought that the quality of a person's faith is fully tested. Most of the time we can survive without too much difficulty. Two people – a man and his wife, perhaps – may both profess to have faith in God; and who is to say how genuine that faith may be? But, when the drought comes, she may survive because her trust has been deeply rooted in Christ, and he may succumb because his profession of faith has really been only a disguise for his self-reliance. He believed in God but he did not depend on God. There is a world of difference between the two.

4. *How can we know ourselves?*

We may well ask how we can be sure that our faith is of the genuine variety. One way is by waiting to see how we respond under pressure but we should not need to wait that long. We want to be sure in advance that our faith will hold when the temptations come.

An important clue is to be found in the verses which follow the parable of the two trees, especially verses 9 and 14. Verse 9 speaks of the desperate condition of the human heart without God's grace: 'The heart is deceitful above all things, and desperately corrupt; who can understand it?' And then it goes on 'I the Lord search the mind and try (or test) the heart'.

The first step to finding a true faith is to recognize one's own utter helplessness. 'Desperately corrupt' sounds a little dramatic to our ears but translate it 'incurably sick' or 'gravely ill' and the sense is clear. Those who are well have no need of a physician. . . . Only those who are sick call in outside help. There can be no depth of faith unless we begin from a position of despair.

Verse 14 echoes the cry for help. 'Heal me, O Lord, and I shall be healed; save me, and I shall be saved.' They are the words wrung from lips that know there is no other way to find cleansing and salvation. Unless this prayer is answered we are lost.

> Nothing in my hand I bring,
> Simply to thy Cross I cling;
> Naked, come to thee for dress;
> Helpless, look to thee for grace;
> Foul, I to the fountain fly;
> Wash me, Saviour, or I die.

Of the men and women in the gospels who came to Jesus to be

healed, few came upright. They came and knelt before him like
Jairus; they cried out for mercy from afar, like the ten lepers;
they were lowered to the ground at his feet like the paralytic;
they shyly touched the hem of his garment. And the faith that
depends, the faith that relies, is the faith that calls out despair-
ingly but hopefully 'Lord save me, and I shall be saved'.

Prayer: Help us, dear Lord, to know and to accept the fact of our
great need. Without your grace we cannot survive. Without your salvation we are utterly lost. We cast ourselves
upon your mercy. Lord Christ, great Physician, heal our
souls and save us for your mercy's sake. We believe in
you, we depend on you, we belong to you. Amen.

(*Hymns: Rock of Ages, cleft for me; Jesu, lover of my soul; Lord,
save thy world; in bitter need; Lord of all power, I give you my
will.*)

14. FALSE PROPHETS

Jeremiah 23.21,22 '*I did not send the prophets, yet they ran; I did not
speak to them, yet they prophesied. But if they had stood in my
council, then they would have proclaimed my words to my
people, and they would have turned them from their evil way,
and from the evil of their doings.*'

Aim: To understand what the prophets taught about true and
false prophecy and to discover the relevance of that teaching for
the Church today. Reading: Jeremiah 23. 9–32.

I am always impressed by the way in which television experts
can appear on the box and identify genuine antiques from clever
imitations, and then, for good measure, they give you the name
of the craftsman and his life history as well. They modestly say

that it is simply a matter of practice, but I am left feeling envious and incompetent.

The same is true of practised birdwatchers. A distant blob appears on the horizon and they confidently call out 'goldeneye' or 'bar-tailed godwit' while I am still trying to get my binoculars in focus. This secret power of instant identification is called in the trade 'jizz', a word found in no dictionary that I know of, but meaning instinctive recognition based on years of experience. I wish I had more of it.

The people of God in Bible times faced equally difficult problems of identification. How, for instance, do you tell a good man from a charlatan? How can you say whether a prophecy or an utterance purporting to be inspired by the Spirit of God is genuine and true or an exceedingly clever confidence-trick? It was a problem for the New Testament Church as well as for the Old. When travelling preachers came to your city, how could they be identified as being loyal to the apostolic faith, and not purveyors of some plausible heresy?

The Bible abounds in guidelines on this subject*, and Jeremiah 23 is one of the most important chapters dealing with it. When two men, dressed alike and claiming to be prophets of the Lord, speak apparent contradictions, how do you know which one to believe? Jeremiah gives six criteria.

1.   *The test of personal morality*

'In the prophets of Jerusalem I have seen a horrible thing: they commit adultery and walk in lies' (v.14). I have no doubt that this refers to physical rather than spiritual adultery – the context demands it – and that this kind of behaviour was thought by Jeremiah to disqualify a man from speaking God's true word. One suspects that adultery and dishonesty were pretty prevalent in Judah in Jeremiah's day and were not greeted with the same sense of shock and scandal that a more puritanical period of Israel's history would have accorded them. But that does not weaken Jeremiah's stand. His attitude may be summed up as follows:

(a) Low standards of popular morality do not lower the stan-

*Passages include Deuteronomy 13. 1–5; 18. 20–22; Jeremiah 28 and 29; Ezekiel 13; 1 John 4. 1–6.

dards set by God. The seventh and the ninth commandments remain as God's requirements and any infringement is transgression of his law.

(b) The prophets are called not merely to speak God's word but to embody and abide by his laws. Therefore they of all people must be scrupulous in their personal conduct if they are to be credible as his spokesmen and able to discern his word.

(c) Such demanding standards do not ignore the problem of human frailty. Even men of God fall short and disobey God's laws, but they show that they are men of God by their sense of shame and repentance before God. Jeremiah's 'horrible thing' is not that the prophets *have* committed adultery (which is forgivable) but that they *do* commit adultery (which is not).

2. *The test of public influence*

Of these false prophets Jeremiah says: 'They strengthen the hands of evildoers, so that no one turns from his wickedness' (v.14).

The word 'turn' is one of the key verbs in the vocabulary of the Old Testament prophets. In Hebrew *shûbh,* pronounced to rhyme with 'move', it can convey a little or a lot. It can mean simply to turn back, to go home; or, more deliberately, to turn round and go in the opposite direction. It can mean a change of mind, to repent of sin and turn to God. Causatively, it can be used of changing people's ways, converting them. In this latter sense it was one of the prophet's primary tasks. He called men and women to turn from their sinful ways to God, and his success was judged by the measure of repentance that he induced.

So a verdict of 'no one turns from his wickedness' is clear evidence that the man is no true prophet of the Lord.

3. *The test of a conditional gospel*

'Thus says the Lord of hosts: "Do not listen to the words of the prophets who prophesy to you, filling you with vain hopes . . . . They say continually to those who despise the word of the Lord, 'It shall be well with you'; and to everyone who stubbornly follows his own heart, they say, 'No evil shall come upon you.' " ' (vs. 16,17).

There appears to be a contradiction here. The gospel is without any doubt a gospel of peace – God and sinners reconciled. Its preachers have the task of proclaiming this good news to all and sundry. There is a strong 'it-shall-be-well-with-you' element in all Christian proclamation. That corresponds to the almond branch of Jeremiah's call. God is at work, bringing life and hope, healing and salvation.

But the gospel is never unconditional. Grace may be free (yes, grace certainly *is* free) but it is only to be found at ground level, at the foot of the Cross. There is no *word* of grace for those who despise or try to sidestep the *place* of grace.

The false prophet is so anxious to leap in with the good news that he bypasses the need for repentance, and the message he proclaims becomes a false gospel. It lulls the conscience instead of pricking it. It induces a sense of security without first bringing a sense of sin. It fails to deal with the root problem of the human heart and so, although initially it may console the hearer, it ultimately defrauds him of the gift of forgiveness.

4. *The test of spirituality*

Verse 18 introduces us to another important Hebrew word, the noun *sôdh* (rhyming with 'loathe'). It is rendered 'council' in RSV, but it has a variety of meanings. In Psalm 25.14 it is the *friendship* of the Lord which is for those who fear him, and he makes known to them his covenant. Proverbs 3.32 tells us that though the perverse man is an abomination to the Lord, the upright are in his *confidence*. Amos says: 'Surely the Lord God does nothing without revealing his *secret* to his servants the prophets' (Amos 3.7).

So the word suggests God's inner circle of intimates, advisers, confidants; those who spend time in his presence, who learn his secrets, who listen to his voice. No man can be a true prophet unless he spends a considerable time in the secret place with his Lord. That is where the word of the Lord is to be discovered.

5. *The test of theology*

Here I refer to verses 23 and 24, which deal with the character of God. There are two points worthy of note.

(a) The right balance in our understanding of God. 'Am I a God at hand, says the Lord, and not a God afar off?' (23). Two errors are to be avoided – on the one hand, making God remote, impersonal, distant, and not allowing him to be our loving Father; and on the other hand so bringing him down to earth that we get positively 'chummy' with him and forget that he is Lord of the universe as well. Both extremes are equally suspect. The balanced path is a delicate one between the two.

(b) The right humility before an all-seeing God. 'Can a man hide himself in secret places so that I cannot see him? says the Lord' (24). We are all accountable to God – the true prophet and the false prophet alike, the saint and the sinner. God sees us and knows us at our best and at our worst. Only when we realize that will we be able to serve him responsibly.

6. *The test of the quality of the message*

In Jeremiah's view there was a world of difference between dreams and oracles. Perhaps that was because dreams called forth skills of ingenious interpretation, whereas oracles came to men through prayer and the intelligent use of their minds. Jeremiah was a great believer in allowing a word from the Lord to 'brew up' in his mind, as he worked on it, applied it and finally uttered it. A spurious prophecy was like straw, blown away with a puff of wind, of no lasting value to anyone. A true word was like wheat, with the seed of life within it, capable of growing and finding its way through hard-packed earth, a fruitful force to be reckoned with. Or like fire. Or like a hammer smiting heart and conscience and breaking up the toughest opposition.

Here then are the tests of true prophecy. Few sermons and fewer preachers will reach such high standards. But they represent the ideals by which we judge our ministry, the goals for which we aim and the standards from which we fall short.

Prayer: Teach us, Lord, to recognize your word and to submit to it and, from all the many voices that we hear, to pick out the voice of the Spirit and to receive it into our hearts.
(*Hymns: Lord, thy word abideth; Come, gracious Spirit, heavenly Dove; Thanks to God whose Word was spoken.*)

15. THE NEW COVENANT

Jeremiah 31. 31–34 *'Behold, the days are coming, says the Lord, when I will make a new covenant with the house of Israel and the house of Judah. . . . I will put my law within them, and I will write it upon their hearts; and I will be their God, and they shall be my people. And no longer shall each man teach his neighbour and each his brother, saying, "Know the Lord", for they shall all know me, from the least of them to the greatest, says the Lord; for I will forgive their iniquity, and I will remember their sin no more.'*

Aim: To illuminate the relationship between the believer and God which is confirmed and renewed in the Holy Communion service. This sermon will be found to be particularly appropriate on Passion Sunday, when Jeremiah 31.31–34 is read at the Eucharist.

This passage has been described by John Bright as the high point of Jeremiah's theology and as 'one of the profoundest and most moving passages in the Bible'. It is quoted in full in Hebrews 8.8–12 and again more briefly in Hebrews 10.16–17. Echoes of it are found in other parts of the New Testament, not least in the great Institution narrative – 'This cup is the new covenant in my blood' (Luke 22.20; 1 Cor.11.25).

Jeremiah's words are not the first indication that all is not well with God's relationship with Israel. For years past the prophets have been accusing God's people of backsliding, idolatry, spiritual adultery and wilful disobedience. You might have expected that all these denunciations would culminate in a word from God to say that he was finishing with his people for ever. Instead, something better is announced: a new covenant is going to be made.

But what is, or was, a covenant? It has nothing to do with the pink string and sealing-wax of present day legal transactions or property transfers, still less with tax benefits for charitable giving. In Old Testament times, a covenant was an agreement, a relationship, an undertaking. Wherever two people entered into obligations to one another – through a promise, a commercial transaction, an act of hospitality or a marriage ceremony – they were said to be in covenant. No documents needed to be signed:

the witnessed word was enough. So it was not surprising to find God's relationship with Israel described in covenant language from the very earliest days.

What happened on Mount Sinai then was that Israel was given a code of laws, the Ten Commandments, through Moses their leader. It contained God's requirements for their behaviour towards him and towards their fellow-men; it assured them that the Lord would always be their God and they would be uniquely the Lord's people, and as they accepted this new way a covenant was made.

From time to time this covenant was reasserted, sometimes it was enlarged or made more specific. For instance, in David's reign, the prophet Nathan is credited with having elaborated the covenant to include a special clause relating to David's offspring as Israel's royal line (2 Samuel 7). Jeremiah's chief claim to fame was that he foretold a new style of covenant, based not upon outward observances and codified laws but upon a change of heart leading to spontaneous obedience and the ready response of mind and will. This new covenant had many of the features of what went before it: the partners were still the Lord and his people, the general aim was not markedly different, the blessings that were promised were much the same. But it followed a different method.

First, the new covenant was to be *personal and individual,* not national and corporate. Internalizing the covenant means personalizing it as well. God makes it with 'me' as well as with 'us'. It is done on a heart-to-heart basis: 'I will write it upon their hearts' (verse 33).

Secondly, the new covenant was to be *inward and spiritual,* and not simply a matter of outward observance. 'I will put my law within them' is a far cry from commandments engraved upon stone tablets. It suggests that there is to be an instinctive recognition of God's requirements, an informed conscience, a heightened moral sense.

Thirdly, the new covenant appears to be *designed for all* and not just for some. Is there in verse 34 a hint that the laws of God will no longer be the preserve of Israel, but will be recognized and followed universally? 'No longer shall each man teach his neighbour and each his brother, saying, "Know the Lord", for they shall all know me, from the least of them to the greatest, says the

Lord". Certainly this was how the New Testament writers understood these words.

So, in the light of our Lord's words in the upper room, when he took the cup and spoke of the new covenant in his blood, we can add the crowning difference between the old and the new – the old was sealed in the never-ending round of sacrificial victims, but the new was *sealed once for all in the precious blood of Christ*. These are the four significant differences between the two covenants and they are underlined for us every time we attend a celebration of the Lord's Supper.

For instance, although we are part of a large congregation we come to receive the bread and the wine one by one. We eat and drink physically, but we feed on Christ inwardly in our souls. The invitation to draw near is not restricted to members of a select group or a chosen race; like the kingdom of heaven, it is open to all believers. The only condition that is imposed is spiritual preparedness or repentance. The words from the 1662 Prayer Book cannot be bettered: 'Ye that do truly and earnestly repent you of your sins, and are in love and charity with your neighbours, and intend to lead a new life, following the commandments of God, and walking from henceforth in his holy ways; draw near with faith. . . .' Within the limits of such an invitation, all may come to receive Christ's gift of himself. Though a particular Church may have its own rules of admission to Holy Communion we must beware lest our regulations turn into a denominational legalism and we sit light to the standards of spiritual intention – repentance and faith – which are the demands that Christ makes of those who worship him. If we come in the right frame of mind we can go away with the promise of God through Jeremiah ringing in our ears: I will forgive your iniquity and I will remember your sin no more (verse 34).

Prayer: We thank you, Lord Jesus Christ, for the new covenant in your blood. Write your law upon our hearts and make us new, that we may worship you, obey you and feed upon you day by day.

(*Hymns: Lord, enthroned in heavenly splendour; Once, only once, and once for all; Bread of heaven, on thee we feed.*)

16. BY THE WATERS OF BABYLON

Ezekiel 1.1 *'The heavens were opened, and I saw visions of God.'*

Aim: To introduce the congregation to the strange figure of Ezekiel and to teach what he understood of the nature of God. It is advisable to read at least part of chapter 1 as the Old Testament lesson.

Ezekiel is not the most popular prophet in the Old Testament to preach about. Some would dismiss him and say that he was mad. The Rabbis used to say that no one under the age of thirty should be allowed to read his prophecy. So he has been abandoned to the trivializers and the allegorists to make what they like of him, and few have been able to dispute with them. It is hardly surprising therefore that von Daniken's outrageous theories about spacemen and flying saucers have come in to fill the vacuum left by decades of avoiding the real Ezekiel and his message.

1. Who was Ezekiel?

He was a priest, trained in all the secrets of the temple, its worship and its symbolism. He was an exile, dispossessed from home and homeland by the invading Babylonian armies and resettled in the deserts of modern Iraq along with thousands of his fellow countrymen. He was a young man, probably in his twenties, and so unable to fulfil his life's ambition to serve as a priest in Jerusalem. But his faith had not died, and he was called in his vision to be a prophet of God's word and to minister to his people in their hour of need. God never leaves his flock without a shepherd.

2. Vision

It began with a vision. A dark storm-cloud from the north drew near and began to gleam with fire and lightning. Then came the description of God's throne, mounted upon strange winged creatures, all dazzlingly bright, their wings whirring loudly, and with wheels that touched the ground and that moved incessantly in every direction. It defies understanding or logical explanation. The Lord who is seated upon the throne is scarcely distinguishable in the blazing light that surrounded him. The whole picture is awesome and terrifying.

That of course is its message. God *is* inscrutable, unknowable, breathtakingly beyond description. He cannot be approached too closely or gazed upon or charted or docketed. He is the great and sovereign Lord, beyond time and space, dauntingly different. But, more than that, he is infinitely mobile (those wheels!) and he makes his presence known even in the God-forsaken wastes of Babylonia. He is much more than a localized God of a Jerusalem temple. His territory includes these foreign parts: so not even exile can separate his people from his care.

'Whither shall I go from thy Spirit? Or whither shall I flee from thy presence? If I ascend to heaven, thou art there! If I make my bed in Sheol, thou art there! If I take the wings of the morning and dwell in the uttermost parts of the sea, even there thy hand shall lead me, and thy right hand shall hold me' (Psalm 139.7–10).

3. *Voice*

Ezekiel, like so many before and after him, fell on his face before the vision of God. Like Moses at the burning bush, he felt as if he were standing on holy ground. He had nothing to say. His eyes were to the ground, unable to face the prospect of looking at God's splendour. His legs felt like jelly. All he could do was listen for God to speak. 'And he said to me, Son of man, stand upon your feet, and I will speak with you' (2.1).

'Son of man' was Ezekiel's favourite description of himself. It had not yet become a messianic title. It simply meant 'member of the human race'; not a person set apart. Just himself. Before God we are all just 'sons of men', because God chooses what is weak in the world to shame the strong, so that no human being might boast in his presence. Nonentities are more useful to God than celebrities.

The voice spoke a word of reassurance and then of commissioning. 'Son of man, I send you to the people of Israel, to a nation of rebels, who have rebelled against me.' It was a missionary call, but not overseas and with no language-barrier to cross. Instead there would be the immense barrier of wilful disobedience to break through. 'The house of Israel will not listen to you: for they are not willing to listen to me; because all the house of Israel are of a hard forehead and of a stubborn heart' (3.7). This is the hardest resistance to deal with. Words bounce back without making any impact: not even affection produces a response of tenderness or gratitude. There is to be apathy, total refusal to listen or to change.

But God does promise Ezekiel the wherewithal to deal with the problem – in terms, not of a winning manner or a silvery tongue, but of a hard head! I suspect that the gift of the Spirit needed by most Christian workers today is not one of those listed in Romans or 1 Corinthians, but the gift of toughness, of resilience, the ability to survive discouragement and to keep on in the face of an unresponsive congregation. The temptation is to ask for a move, to seek a more fulfilling ministry, but that solves nothing. God's gift is a thicker-than-usual skin – and a sensitive soul like Ezekiel certainly needed it.

4. *Message*

In a strange piece of symbolism the Lord then gives Ezekiel a scroll of writing and tells him to eat it. This is meant to refer to the prophet's message to the people, and the contents of the scroll were 'words of lamentation and mourning and woe'. But when he ate it, he said that 'it was in my mouth as sweet as honey' (3.3).

Presumably we have here the paradox of an unpopular message which nevertheless becomes acceptable to the preacher because he is obedient to his call and commission. Because it is God's message, he relishes it and delights to do God's will. We can also see the importance of feeding our souls on God's truth as the best and only way of preparing for a lifetime of ministry and service for him. Read, mark, learn and inwardly digest it! The more we read our Bible the more we will develop a taste for it, and the sweeter it will become.

Well, whatever happened to Ezekiel when he saw visions of God, it was a devastating experience for him. He said he 'went in bitterness in the heat of my spirit, the hand of the Lord being strong upon me . . . and I sat there overwhelmed among them seven days' (3.14f.). Like Paul after his Damascus road experience, he needed time to adjust and to recover from the shock of it all. Then the message came again, and this time it was to say that his task was to be a watchman to the house of Israel, warning, staying awake, standing between a sleeping population and the dangers outside.

The Christian Church has a watchman's role, though rarely does it exercise it. Perhaps we are too concerned to get involved with society, working to change and improve its structures from within, forgetting that the whole world is under God's judgement and needs to turn to him to repent. The wicked needs to be warned of the eternal consequences of his sins, and the righteous needs to be warned for fear he lapses into a dangerous complacency. The watchman's work is never done. But it is desperately necessary if the city is to be saved.

Here then is Ezekiel's God, alive and free in the place of his people's captivity; not deserting them but reassuring them; calling out his spokesman, to lead and teach the people. A God of splendour, of majesty, of holiness. A God who warns, who confronts, who dismays. A God who uses one young man (no more) and redirects his life to be a prophet of the Lord and a watchman to his people.

Prayer: Give us, Lord, a vision of your greatness, bigger than all our dreams, far beyond all our imaginings. And with the vision may we hear the voice that calls us and sends us out to do your bidding and to serve you in the world.
(Hymns: Hark, 'tis the watchman's cry; O come, O come, Emmanuel; The advent of our King.)

17. LOVE SONGS

Ezekiel 33.32 *'You are to them like one who sings love songs with a beautiful voice and plays well on an instrument, for they hear what you say, but they will not do it.'*

Aim: To underline the importance of obeying God's word and not merely listening to it. This would have special relevance for those using the ASB lections on the third Sunday before Lent, when the theme is 'Christ the Teacher'.

Anyone who has teenage children knows what it is like to have the incessant sound of a stereo playing cassettes or records most of the day and half-way into the night. It makes many a parent pine for the day when houses were built of more substantial material and with attics. The words in any case are usually indistinct and take second place to the beat and the musical backing. When the words can be identified on a record sleeve, one is sometimes grateful that they are so indecipherable.

It seems strange that as many as two and a half thousand years ago the pop-singer of Ezekiel's day was being called into service to illustrate a similar point about audibility and impact. True, the words of our text befit a minstrel-singer more than an electronically-dominated rock group, but the similarity still exists. What do they sound like, what are they saying, and what effect do they have on those who hear? The questions are still the same.

Ezekiel had no objection to the words of the ballads he heard sung, though no one could accuse him of being sympathetic to sentimentalism. Prophets are rarely found among the ranks of the romantics. He was a man of God's word and a man with a message. His only concern was to speak the truth and to make men believe it and repent or mend their ways or whatever was needed. So, like every good evangelist, he preached for a verdict.

He doesn't actually blame the pop-culture of his day – and one wonders how far it had infiltrated the internment camps of Babylonia anyway – but he is scornful of the way in which people can be immunized by words to the meaning of words. 'They hear what you say, but they will not do it.' Perhaps that was a reflection of his own frustration at not being listened to. If so, the problem is not his alone. Every preacher and every prophet has agonized over why it is that the message which is so self-evident to him does not produce a ready response in his hearers.

1. *Herod*

The relationship between Herod and John the Baptist is a case in point. You would have expected them to be sworn enemies, and it is certainly true that John did not go out of his way to curry favour with the Tetrarch of Judea. Instead of offering some private counselling session he said to Herod openly and bluntly, 'It is not lawful for you to have your brother's wife'. End of message. Which meant that everyone knew exactly where they stood: Herod in the wrong, Herodias in a fury and John the Baptist in prison. But then St Mark goes on to tell us that 'Herod feared John, knowing that he was a righteous and holy man, and kept him safe. When he heard him, he was much perplexed; and yet he heard him gladly' (Mark 6.20).

Here in this graphic episode you have the conflict of a man with a guilty conscience, attracted to the preaching of righteousness because he knows it is what he needs, yet lacking the moral courage to repent and to change his ways. The result: he gave way to Salome's request and John was silenced for ever. Except in so far as he went on speaking to Herod's conscience. 'They hear what you say, but they will not do it.'

2. *Felix*

Another example is Felix, the Roman governor of Judea, who arrested Paul and kept him in prison for two years without trial, hoping for a handsome bribe to be offered for his release. Listen to how St Luke describes their relationship: 'Felix sent for Paul and heard him speak upon faith in Christ Jesus. And as he argued about justice and self-control and future judgement, Felix was alarmed and said, "Go away for the present; when I have an opportunity I will summon you". . . . So he sent for him often and conversed with him. But when two years had elapsed, Felix was succeeded by Porcius Festus; and desiring to do the Jews a favour, Felix left Paul in prison' (Acts 24.24–27).

Once again, the preacher of the truth was not without his attractions. There was a magnetism about the man and a compelling quality about the message that he proclaimed. But the word needs to be believed for it to be of any value, and as far as Herod and Felix were concerned it only confirmed their condemnation. As the writer to the Hebrews put it, 'The message which they heard did not benefit them, because it did not meet with faith in the hearers' (Heb.4.2).

3. *The Sower*

Maybe Ezekiel would have been encouraged if he had been given a preview of the parable of the sower. This was our Lord's definitive statement about the effect of preaching the word of

God. No guaranteed success-story here. Thorns choking the growth, stony ground stunting it, birds of the air preventing its germination. Only one in four does well and produces the harvest. The seed is undeniably good seed, but three parts of it are wasted; and I don't think the sower is entirely to blame. The parable should really be called 'the parable of the soils' because that is what it is all about. What kind of soil are you? Shallow, stony, or receptive? 'He who has ears to hear, let him hear.'

I sometimes think that our emphasis in evangelism is all wrong. We take great pains with our message, with our missions and with our methods, but should we not be spending more time in preparing the ground so that the gospel when preached will find responsive hearers? This means a greater concentration on education, on family life, on the right use of the media, where attitudes are formed and character is developed. The shallow soil is usually a sign of a shallow personality. The rapacious birds of the air are the hostile influences to which the hearer is vulnerable. Thank God, it is not always so, or we ourselves might never have come to faith; but it is partly true.

The message applies not only to the unevangelized, but to the Christian too. It was to his followers that Jesus told the parable of the sheep and the goats. 'Not everyone who says to me "Lord, Lord", shall enter the kingdom of heaven, but he who does the will of my Father who is in heaven.' For as we do it to one of the least of these his brethren, we do it to him. James underlines the same teaching in his own distinctive way: 'Be doers of the word, and not hearers only, deceiving yourselves. . . . He who looks into the perfect law, the law of liberty, and perseveres, being no hearer that forgets but a doer that acts, he shall be blessed in his doing' (James 1.22,25).

The call is to the Church to hear and to obey, to practise what our teachers preach. We all fall short and we all need to mend our ways. It has been said that the Church preaches unity and practises disunity, that it preaches equality and practises inequality, that it preaches love and practises indifference. Perhaps that is why we cut so little ice in this our generation.

So we must be down on our knees to confess our sins; we must learn a greater sensitivity to what God's Word has to say to us. Above all we must learn that simplest but most difficult of lessons that was given us by the Lord's mother at the wedding in

Cana of Galilee. 'Whatsoever he saith unto you, do it.' It is either that, or back to those love-songs that mean not a thing.

Prayer: Teach us, Lord, to listen and to obey, to be doers of the word and not hearers only.

(**Hymns:** *Dear Lord and Father of Mankind; Souls of men! why will ye scatter; O Jesus, I have promised.*)

18.   FOUR STAGES IN SPIRITUAL RENEWAL

Ezekiel 37.3 *'Son of man, can these bones live?'*

Aim: To illustrate some of the qualities which must be found in the life of the local church if renewal is to take place. The sermon would be suitable for Pentecost. It could also form the framework of a series of four sermons, as each point is given more leisurely treatment, during the Easter season. Read in preparation the whole of Ezekiel 37.

I cannot read this wonderful chapter of Ezekiel's vision of the valley of dry bones without my mind going back to a Sunday morning in Holy Trinity, Eastbourne, when it was read as the first lesson by a well-built gentleman wearing a splendid gold chain of office. I knew he was not the mayor, and eventually the notices informed us that the church was acting as host to the chairman and members of the National Conference of the Meat-Traders Federation! I cannot believe that they chose the lessons, nor that the vicar had his tongue in his cheek, so I must assume that the lectionary was to blame.

The passage itself has its whimsical moments, not least when the prophet has to answer the Lord's question, 'Can these bones live?' 'Lord, thou knowest' must go down in religious literature as one of the most diplomatic answers to an obviously loaded question.

At the same time the episode is exceptionally searching and speaks deeply to generations of readers, both Jewish and Christian, just as it did many years ago to the prophet Ezekiel. Ezekiel, you will recall, was hundreds of miles away from his beloved Jerusalem, an exile in the desert wastes of Babylonia, when God appeared to him and called him to be a prophet. God gave him a vision of his glory and then commissioned him to be a preacher with, in effect, the familiar words, 'Receive the cure of souls which is both yours and mine'. And Ezekiel waited to hear what parish he was going to be given. And the Lord said: 'I am sending you to the people of Israel, to a nation of rebels. . . . They are impudent and stubborn; I send you to them: and you shall say to them "Thus says the Lord God". And whether they hear or refuse to hear they will know that there has been a prophet among them.' What a first living to be offered!

For five years and for thirty-six chapters Ezekiel preached the word to them. The only impression he gained was that they were becoming harder and harder, more and more resistant to his words.

Then came the second vision. It was probably given to him in the very spot where first he had received his call: a fold in the plain to which he used to go for quiet and for prayer. A sacred place, where he could remember and be refreshed, or where he could wrestle with the problems that beset him. In imagination he looked out over the desert plain and, instead of rocks and boulders, it seemed as if the place was littered with armour and clothing and bones – the wreckage of a battlefield two weeks after the event, when there was nothing left to interest even a starving vulture. And God said to Ezekiel: 'Does this remind you of anthing?' and he said: 'Yes, Lord, my parish!'

But can these bones live? Can stubborn, self-pitying Israel ever come to life again? Can your parish, which is so turned in on itself, so set in its ways, so backward-looking, can it come alive? Like us, Ezekiel hadn't the nerve to say No but he hadn't the faith to say Yes. 'Lord, thou knowest' was all he could muster.

Perhaps there was just sufficient faith in those three words to encourage God to continue the conversation, and to point the way to the four stages of spiritual renewal which is our theme today.

1. *Prophesy to these bones*

Ezekiel's first duty was to persist in the ministry to which God had called him. Renewal does not come through an abandonment of our basic responsibilities. The prophet is called to keep on prophesying, not to try some new technique in the hope that it will prove more effective. The only proviso is that he must prophesy in hope. Listen to these words from verse 5: 'Thus says the Lord God to these bones: Behold . . . . you shall live.'

In the film of John Wesley's life which was made by J. Arthur Rank for the Methodist Church in the United States, there is a moving scene where, with his new-found Moravian friends, Wesley is trying to minister to a condemned criminal on his way to the gallows. His platitudes fall on deaf ears. Then one of the Moravian pastors pleads with Wesley: 'Brother John, preach faith until you have faith'. Wesley had not yet come to the place where his heart was strangely warmed by the reading of Luther's preface to Romans, but he was being asked to preach what he had not yet discovered for himself.

In the same way, Ezekiel saw no inconsistency in being called to preach revival when he was not even sure that it could or would ever come.

2. *Prophesy to the wind*

The words 'breath' and 'wind' and 'spirit' are one and the same in Hebrew. Prophesying to the wind means calling upon the Spirit of God to 'breathe upon these slain that they may live'. It is a separate activity from stage one. It is directed not to the bones but the four winds of heaven, to the Breath of God. It speaks to us not of preaching but of praying.

So the miracle in this vision is performed in two stages. First the prophesying, which caused the bones to come together and the flesh and the skin to cover them; then the praying, which brought the Spirit of God into the lifeless bodies and set them up on their feet like an exceeding great army.

3. *One in my hand*

Most sermons on Ezekiel 37 end here, but there is more to follow. The vision is followed by another word from the Lord consisting of a brief enacted parable. Take two sticks, says God, one for Judah and the other for Israel, and hold them in the palm of your hand so that they look like one stick – and learn the importance that I attach to the unity of my people.

When a church is revived and experiences new life, there comes the urgent need to safeguard and to cultivate unity. Renewal movements have been known to split churches in two, but that is never God's intention. They must work for harmony and reconciliation between clergy and laity, between young and old, between the traditionalist and the progressive elements in the congregation. This is much less spectacular than the miracle-working preaching or praying, but it is of the essence of church life: it is the fellowship of the Holy Spirit. There will never be true renewal in the Spirit unless the church's leaders and members are endeavouring to keep the unity of the Spirit in the bond of peace – and that means much more than handshakes or hugs at the Eucharist.

4. *One Shepherd*

The chapter concludes with a forward look to the age of the Messiah. 'They shall all have one shepherd. They shall follow my ordinances and be careful to observe my statutes . . . and David my servant shall be their prince for ever . . . . My dwelling-place shall be with them; and I will be their God, and they shall be my people' (verses 24–27).

What does this add to the teaching of the chapter? Isn't it that the renewed church, the revived army, finds its completion only as it submits its life to the Lordship of Christ? In the Good Shepherd's care, in the reign of the Prince of Peace, in the sovereign rule of Christ, the church will know the consummation of its life here on earth, and it will become fully alive.

Here then are four identifiable ingredients in bringing a dead church to life again. The ministry of the word – clear, hopeful, expectant; the ministry of the Spirit – by prayer and by persistence; the ministry of reconciliation – uniting, welding, harmonizing; and submission to the Church's Lord in every respect. Only so can dead bones live.

Prayer: Holy Spirit of God, breathe into our hearts and give us life; break down our divisions and make us one; lead us to Jesus that we may follow him and serve him as our King.

*(Hymn: Revive thy work, O Lord; O Holy Ghost, thy people bless;
Breathe on me, Breath of God; Filled with the Spirit's power,
with one accord.)*

19. THE RIVER OF LIFE

Ezekiel 47.9 *'So everything will live where the river goes'*.

Aim: To draw on the symbolism of the river of life in order to
teach about the work of the Spirit in the life of the Christian and
of the Church. The first twelve verses of Ezekiel 47 need to be
read as a lesson, if the context is to be rightly understood.

A river has a fascination for everyone. It speaks to us of tranquillity; it abounds in wild life; it has its own varieties of grasses and
flowers. We can sit by a river bank the whole day long and there
is always something to interest, something new or unexpected.
A rising fish, a beautiful damselfly, a pair of yellow wagtails, a
water-vole.

A river has a long history of symbolism, especially in the
Bible. There are the rivers that watered the Garden of Eden in
Genesis 2 and there is the river of the water of life in Revelation
22. Between Genesis and Revelation the references to rivers, and
even more to water, make for an interesting study.

The Psalmist writes: 'There is a river whose streams make
glad the city of God, the holy habitation of the Most High'
(Psalm 46.4). Joel speaks of mountains dripping sweet wine and
hills flowing with milk 'and all the stream beds of Judah shall
flow with water; and a fountain shall come forth from the house
of the Lord and water the valley of Shittim' (Joel 3.18).
Zechariah, looking forward to the last days, says that 'On that
day living waters shall flow out from Jerusalem, half of them to
the eastern sea and half of them to the western sea (Zech. 14.8).

Our Lord was toying with a similar idea when he said to the
crowds in Jerusalem: 'If anyone thirst, let him come to me and

drink. He who believes in me, as the scripture has said, "Out of his heart shall flow rivers of living water".' And John added, 'Now this he said about the Spirit, which those who believed in him were to receive' (John 7. 37–39).

So there is this good biblical precedent, confirmed by Christ, which likens the life of the Spirit to fresh, flowing water.

The prophet Ezekiel, who began his prophecy by a river in chapter 1, ends with a river in his vision of the restored temple in chapter 47. The first river was a geographical one, named Chebar in Babylonia, a canal near which the prophet and his fellow exiles were encamped as virtual internees and prisoners of Nebuchadnezzar's forces. The last river is an imaginary one, flowing out from beneath the altar of the idealized temple which was designed to replace the one destroyed by those selfsame armies, though with no expectation that it would be built. 'Behold, water was issuing from below the threshold of the temple toward the east . . . . and the water was coming out on the south side' (Ezekiel 47.1f.). If there is symbolism here – and Ezekiel was generally a master of the symbolic – what can it mean?

1. *The source of the river is the temple*

There are two possible symbols here. The first is that the river of life flows out from the temple, the place of God's presence, and this speaks to us of the practice of worship and prayer from which the life of the Spirit finds its source and origin. There is no river without a temple. We cannot expect the Spirit of God to refresh and irrigate our souls unless we practise the presence of God at the start of the day and meet with God in worship at the start of the week.

The second symbol takes this further. The river is said to begin specifically by the altar. Now the altar was the place of sacrifice, where atonement was made for the forgiveness of sins. The Christian counterpart to the Jewish altar is the Cross, and it is from the Cross of Christ that the blessing flows: the preaching of the Cross, the message of sins forgiven, and the life of sacrifice and reconciliation. If the temple and the Cross are central in our lives, the river will flow and where the river goes everything will live.

2. *The direction of the river is towards the wilderness*

Listen to Ezekiel's words again: 'This water flows towards the eastern region and goes down into the Arabah (i.e. towards the Dead Sea); and when it enters the stagnant waters of the sea, the water will become fresh. And wherever the river goes every living creature which swarms will live, and there will be very many fish' (Ezekiel 47.8f.).

The Dead Sea region was a byword for impossibility – infertile, inhospitable, virtually uninhabitable. Yet it was in this direction that God's river flowed. Now this says a great deal to those who are called to live and work in unrewarding jobs, where the response is small and encouragements are few. Someone put it this way: 'God may live in a garden, but he works in a wilderness'. He prefers to take on the intractable rather than to relax in the place that is undemanding.

So the motto for the Christian minister is 'Go for the impossible; that is where God's Spirit goes'. The river flowed towards the east. We are in good company when we tackle the wilderness.

3. *The river begins small and grows as it flows*

Where the water flowed from below the threshold of the temple, it began as the merest trickle. A rare Hebrew word is used in verse 2 and it is found elsewhere only in the word for a 'flask'. The connecting link is that as the flask is tilted its contents dribble out on to the ground. It is this verb 'to dribble' or 'trickle' which is found here of the river beginning to emerge from the temple.

But as it flows it gets deeper. After a thousand cubits it is ankle-deep; another thousand cubits and it is knee-deep; another thousand and it is up to one's waist; another thousand and 'it was a river that I could not pass through, for the waters had risen; it was deep enough to swim in, a river that could not be passed through. And he said to me, "Son of man, have you seen this?" ' (47.5f.). What did Ezekiel make of it though?

He does not say so in so many words. But I think Ezekiel would have understood the symbolism of God's ever-deepening love, the Spirit's ever-intensifying power. That whereas human life from childhood to old age is a story of ever-diminishing resources, life with Christ is a series of ever-increasing blessings. The older we grow, the richer we become.

It is encouraging also to notice that God often begins with a trickle. Most great movements of God's Spirit grow from small beginnings, sometimes from quite small and insignificant people whom he trains up until they are able to swim in deep water, to launch out from the shallows in his name. Like the servant in the parable to whom the master said, 'Well done, good and faithful servant; you have been faithful over a little, I will set you over much; enter into the joy of your master' (Matt. 25.23). Do not despise the day of small things – nor the small people that God is bringing on! The river begins small and grows as it flows.

Every Christian worker, then, should plan for growth and look for growth in the work that he does. What is at present a wilderness can be transformed into a garden. The landscape can be altered, grass and trees can fill the waste ground, a desert can be turned into a fruitful field where 'their fruit will be for food and their leaves for healing'. All things are possible with God, and we must rely on him to give the increase.

This is more than mere symbolism. It is more than a picture of what may be. We should claim it by faith and believe that it is a promise of what *will* be. And our Christian lives and our Christian service will be marked by the motto: 'Everything will live where the river goes'.

Prayer: Fill us, Lord, with your Holy Spirit, and let his life flow through us to the blessing and enrichment and healing of others.

(*Hymns: Like a river glorious is God's perfect peace; Revive they work, O Lord! I hunger and I thirst*)

20. A MORNING CLOUD

Hosea 6.4. *'What shall I do with you, O Ephraim? What shall I do with you, O Judah? Your love is like a morning cloud, like the dew that goes early away.'*

Aim: To stimulate the hearers to a deeper and more lasting love for God. There is no occasion when this would not be appropriate, but the passage (Hosea 6. 1–6) is read in the ASB lectionary on Rogation Sunday (Easter 5) in alternate years.

The name of 'Morning Cloud' must be familiar to every Englishman who has the slightest knowledge either of politicians or of ocean-going racing. It would be interesting to discover if Mr Edward Heath was aware of our text when he named his famous yacht. I would imagine that in his mind at any rate the name was intended to be a sign of hope, though the context of Hosea's original message sounded a note of despair. In spite of all their protestations of faith and loyalty, Israel's love was 'like a morning cloud', vanishing with the dew on a sunny day.

Hosea's theme can be summed up in the simple message 'There is a love that fades and there is a love that lasts: which love is yours?' Love was always his subject, God's love for his people, the people's love for God, Hosea's love for his wife and hers for him. He learnt about it the hard way – through his wife's unfaithfulness. Let me sketch in the background.

1. *Hosea's marriage*

The lady's name was Gomer. Some have supposed that she was a prostitute from the very beginning and they quote the opening words of his prophecy: 'The Lord said to Hosea, "Go, take to yourself a wife of harlotry and have children of harlotry, for the land commits great harlotry by forsaking the lord".' Now, quite apart from the moral problem of the Lord telling a prophet to marry a prostitute, we have to say that this does not follow at all. To the Hebrew the phrase 'a wife of harlotry' can mean simply that that is how she ended up. It is no judgement on her initial purity. Indeed the greater likelihood is that she was pure as a bride and that their love for each other was true and honourable. This interpretation fits much better with the parable which Hosea is going to make out of his experience.

They had their children, three of them, two boys and a girl, and Hosea gave them symbolical names: Jezreel, Not-pitied, and Not-my-people, which could hardly have helped the marriage! Hosea however was a prophet with a one-track mind when it came to the messages he wanted to convey.

Then Gomer went wrong, as they say, and played fast and

loose. Hosea was humiliated, infuriated and was minded to turn his back on her for ever. Then he remembered the love of God for his people, Israel. Just as he (Hosea) had chosen Gomer to be his bride, so the Lord had chosen Israel as the partner of his love. Israel too had played the harlot and been hopelessly faithless to her God, but God had not for that reason cast her off. He still loved her and wooed her and wanted her love. Could not Hosea do the same for Gomer, the mother of his children? So Hosea goes searching for his lost love and buys her back from the man who has possessed her. It cost him fifteen shekels of silver and fifteen sacks of barley, about the price of a slave, though to Hosea she was worth much more.

Here then is how the prophet's marriage and the prophet's message intertwine. Because it was born out of personal experience it carried a power that no mere story could ever have achieved. A word that comes from the heart and has been lived before it is spoken can be quite irresistible.

There is a love that fades and there is a love that lasts. What is our love for God like? There is usually a correlation between the way we love God and how we relate to other people. A capacity for deep human relationships enables us to love God deeply; shallow friendships reflect a shallow spirituality, But it can change. Our love for God deepens and mellows and we find that every human contact grows in quality as a result.

2.   A Love that Fades

Look at the way the prophet portrays the wrong kind of love. 'In their distress they seek me, saying, "Come, let us return to the Lord; for he has torn that he may heal us; he has stricken, and he will bind us up".' (Hosea 6.1). It reads like a perfectly genuine repentance and turning to God. But it ends with the sad words of our text – 'Your love is like a morning cloud'.

The repentance was too sudden to be real. It was prompted by momentary distress and was concerned to produce instant healing. It was not the repentance that comes from a sense of God's holiness and my sinfulness. There was no confession, no sorrow for sin. We have to learn that forgiveness does not come out of a slot-machine: it is usually quite a painful process. On God's side it cost him the sacrifice of the Cross to achieve reconciliation. On man's side it may be free, but it is never cheap. He who is forgiven little loves little – like that morning cloud!

The other hallmark of the wrong kind of love is perfunctory religion. Notice the contrast of these words: 'I desire steadfast love and not sacrifice, the knowledge of God, rather than burnt offerings' (Hosea 6.6). Religious duties can be performed by anybody at the most trifling cost: a few pounds, an hour or so of your time, a modest inconvenience. To call them sacrifices is to stand the word on its head. There is no costliness about such things at all. And if it costs nothing it's usually worth nothing. So if you want to offer a real sacrifice, let it be in terms of a steadfast love that demands your whole life.

3.   *A Love that Lasts*

Here is the love that counts, the kind God is looking for in his children. It is a love that goes on loving even when it is rejected. A love that persists with the Gomers of this world, and that buys them back from the degradation to which they have sunk. It is the quality of love that God has been showing to us all through our lives, from before the time when we were even aware of him. It is the love that draws us to himself, that sends us forth in his service, that prompts us to give ourselves without reserve to him and for his world. It is the love that we see in Jesus.

Hosea cannot get away from it. His fourteen chapters are like a symphony on the theme of God's steadfast love, which contrasts so momentously with our poor love for him. He ends his prophecy with an appeal to his Israelite compatriots: 'Return, O Israel, to the Lord your God, for you have stumbled because of your iniquity' (Hosea 14.1). And he goes on to speak in God's name the kind of words that he had tried so hard to mean as far as Gomer was concerned:

'I will heal their faithlessness; I will love them freely, for my anger has turned from them.

I will be as the dew to Israel; he shall blossom as the lily, he shall strike root as the poplar; his shoots shall spread out; his beauty shall be like the olive, and his fragrance like Lebanon' (Hosea 14. 4–6).

There in the loveliest of language is the tender, steadfast love which we should be showing both to others and to our Lord. There is a love that fades and a love that lasts. What kind of love is ours?

Prayer: Deepen, O Lord, our understanding of your love and let our love be faithful and true. Keep us from all shallowness in our obedience, our faith and our character, and lead us on to know the Lord.

(*Hymns: Gracious Spirit, Holy Ghost; O Love divine, how sweet thou art! O Love that wilt not let me go.*)

21. A PENTECOSTAL CHURCH

Joel 2. 28f *'And it shall come to pass afterward, that I will pour out my spirit on all flesh; your sons and your daughters shall prophesy, your old men shall dream dreams, and your young men shall see visions. Even upon the manservants and maidservants in those days, I will pour out my spirit.'*

Aim: To give the Old Testament background to the events of the first Whitsunday and to put Pentecost in its biblical context.

No one can be sure what actually happened in the upper room in Jerusalem on the day of Pentecost. There was the sound of a rushing mighty wind, the appearance of tongues of fire on the heads of those assembled there, and the speaking with tongues. Why the wind? Why the tongues of fire? How literal and visible and tangible were they? And what was speaking with tongues – inspired gibberish or linguistic genius? We wish we knew what was going on that day.

We do know some of the effects: visitors to Jerusalem heard in their own language about the mighty works of God. Peter and the apostles found themselves preaching Christ with an authority and an impact they had never known before. Conversions followed thick and fast; three thousand were baptized in one day. The Church was being born. And some sneered and gave them twenty-four hours to sober up.

Peter's words were quite clear: 'These men are not drunk, as you suppose . . ., but this is what was spoken by the prophet Joel. . . .' (Acts 2.15f.). Joel will not explain to us the details of what was going on on the day of Pentecost, but he does explain what it all meant, in terms that Peter could identify and the early Church could understand.

1. *The gift of prophecy*

The Holy Spirit was always thought of as the power of God. He came upon people, sometimes quite alarmingly, to give them courage and strength to do battle. He inspired writers and speakers to utter messages from God that had a power of their own within them. He gave supernatural wisdom to judges and to kings or unusual skills to craftsmen like Bezalel (Exodus 31.3), who built the tabernacle. But in the last days, said Joel, God was going to pour out his Spirit upon all men, and the mark of the Spirit would be the gift of prophecy. So what had been reserved to a very few, was now to become the privilege of all. A new age of prophecy and revelation was about to dawn, and in the front rank of those who were to be filled with God's Spirit were fishermen and tax-collectors and ordinary working men, and women as well, no doubt. 'Your sons and your daughters shall prophesy.'

The early Church was a hot-bed of prophesyings. Christians exhorted fellow Christians, ministered in the congregation, spoke with tongues, spoke with assurance, spoke from experience. New truths were discovered daily. It was as if God was renewing his people and opening them up to his Spirit. Those were exciting days to live through, and they began on that famous day of Pentecost – as Joel had foretold. The gift of prophecy had come back.

2. *For all to enjoy*

Whenever the word 'all' is used in Scripture we have to ask ourselves whether it means 'all without distinction' or 'all without exception'. In the case of the later phrase in Joel 2, 'all who call upon the name of the Lord shall be saved', it is obvious that he meant all without exception, and that is certainly how Peter understood it as he preached Christ to the crowds and called them to repentance. Here is the great 'whosoever' of the gospel:

anyone may come and everyone who comes in faith will be received. But the promise to 'pour our my spirit upon all flesh' is more likely to be a case of all without distinction. Instead of restricting the gift of the Spirit to judges and kings and prophets, it is going to be for all sorts of people, high and low, rich and poor, male and female, master and slave, young and old. The Spirit will no longer be reserved for special classes of people. He will be for all to enjoy.

I am not sure that we live by that New Testament doctrine in our church life today. The charismatics are trying to teach us that every Christian has some gift of the Spirit and every gift has to be used in the Body of Christ and for the building up of the Body of Christ, but we are slow to learn it. Sometimes it is the voices of the old men that we stifle, sometimes the voices of young people, sometimes the ministry of women; or else we reject the menservants and the maidservants (the working classes?) and believe them incapable of spiritual leadership. But the Spirit of God is given to the Church for *all* of us to enjoy, and the gift of prophecy is to be found in the most unlikely places.

3. *A new age*

What happened on the day of Pentecost was like a sign to Israel and to the Church, a sign that the age of the Messiah had dawned. That was what Joel was referring to when he spoke of the outpouring of God's Spirit, coupled with that fearsome list of portents about the sun being turned to darkness and the moon into blood before the great and terrible day of the Lord comes. Some of this language was the Old Testament's stock-in-trade for the last days and the day of judgement upon the nations, but it was also the preliminary to a more idyllic life when nations would no longer lift up swords against each other and wild animals would cause no harm, and the golden age would be ushered in.

This is how Peter read the signs of Pentecost. This was to him the beginning of the end-time, the day of the Messiah, the start of a new age. It was what John the Baptist had been referring to when he had said, 'I baptize you with water; but he who is mightier than I is coming, the thong of whose sandals I am not worthy to untie; he will baptize you with the Holy Spirit and with fire' (Luke 3.16). Perhaps that would explain the rushing wind and the tongues of flame in the upper room. It was Luke's way of saying that the Christ had come again. His reign was about to begin.

4. Saved by faith

The watchword of Christ's kingdom is the brief sentence: 'Whoever calls on the name of the Lord shall be saved.' Joel said it and Peter quoted it. It was the gospel-call of the apostles, and before long it was being preached to gentiles as well as to Jews. The Lord was undoubtedly Israel's God, but not exclusively so. He was the God and Father of our Lord Jesus Christ, who had opened the kingdom of heaven to all believers. So Peter invited *all* his hearers to repent and be baptized in the name of Jesus Christ for the forgiveness of their sins so that they too might receive the gift of the Holy Spirit (Acts 2.38). He concluded with the words, 'For the promise is to you and to your children (i.e. all Jews) and to all that are far off (i.e. the gentiles), every one whom the Lord our God calls to him'. God calls us, through the preaching of the apostles. We call upon him, for forgiveness and in faith, and receive his promised salvation. This is the same message that the Church should be preaching to the world today. It has not changed.

How Pentecostal then is our church? we need to ask ourselves. Is there a freedom of the Spirit that releases our tongues to witness and to speak of Christ? Does everyone count and is everyone valued, with their differing gifts and personalities? Are we living as children of the new age, as children of the Kingdom? Does the invitation to come to Christ get through to men and women everywhere, so that they can hear it and sense it and respond to it?

Prayer: Fill us, Lord, with the Spirit of Pentecost that we may burn brightly and speak boldly and live effectively for the sake of your kingdom.

(*Hymns: When God of old came down from heaven; O Holy Ghost, thy people bless; Spirit Divine, attend our prayers; Come, thou Holy Spirit, come.*)

22. 'HIS SERVANTS THE PROPHETS'

Amos 3.7 *'Surely the Lord God does nothing, without revealing his secret to his servants the prophets. The lion has roared; who will not fear? The Lord God has spoken; who can but prophesy?'*

Aim: Taking the example of Amos, to explain the work of an Old Testament prophet and the principles which underlay his ministry and to show their application to the prophetic ministry of the Church.

Although his short book is found in the middle of the prophets in our Bible, Amos is in fact the first of them all. There had been prophets before him but he was the first to have his sayings recorded and written up for later generations to read. He was one of the four prophets of the eighth century before Christ, and we usually think of him as prophesying around the middle of that century, closely followed by Hosea, Isaiah and Micah.

Like many other men of God, Amos was a countryman, a man of the wide open spaces. He herded sheep near Bethlehem, but he used to travel north of the border to Bethel to market his wares – and to preach God's word. But how is it that a farmer could become a prophet of the Lord?

1. *Hearing the Word*

The prophet's first task was to tune in to God, and the lonely silence of the Judean hills was a good place for that to be done. There was a quietness in the air, a grandeur in the scenery and an opportunity to think and to commune with God. Amos was no solitary. He picked up news of what was going on in the world, as his opening chapters bear witness. He could write well and compose oracles in poetic idiom. But above all, he could think, and relate the world he knew to the God he knew. This was how his messages began to take shape. It is how the best sermons still are made.

Make no mistake, Amos was no country bumpkin. His IQ would have impressed anyone, but he knew that God's word was not simply the product of a fertile mind. It had to grow out of a close and living fellowship with his Lord. There had to be an intimacy, a quality of friendship between himself and God which would allow the Lord to tell him his secrets and to share his plans with him.

The prophet was the man who was in that inner circle, as Amos certainly felt himself to be. He had been called to it by God's grace. That was why he would not allow himself to be thought of as a professional. 'I am no prophet', he shouted to the priest at Bethel, 'nor a prophet's son; but I am a herdsman, and a dresser of fig-trees, and the Lord took me from following the flock, and the Lord said to me, "Go, prophesy to my people Israel".' (Amos 7.14f.). He was proud of being a layman, a 'volunteer' whom God had called.

2. *Choosing the Target*

Part of Amos's success as a prophet lay in his selection of what to preach and where to say it. He could have hammered away at idolatry, because Bethel was the town where Israel had set up an alternative temple complete with golden calf, to rival the temple in Jerusalem – but he didn't. He could have charged them with heresy and for establishing a deviant form of the true faith – but he didn't. Instead he hit hard at Israel's sins and particularly the social evils which were a contradiction of God's covenant with his people.

If Amos were here today, what target would be have chosen? Would he have stayed with the pampered luxury of the idle rich? Would he have caned the powerful for their oppression of the poor? Or would he have found some other fault in modern society or in the government of nations or in the Church to take to task? We cannot say. All we can say is that although there were many things he *could* have preached against, he wisely restricted himself to one field and dealt properly with that. Effective preaching needs to be carefully directed at the desired target, and not deflected to lesser issues. Denunciation too widely spread around can lead to the currency being debased.

3. *Speaking the Message*

All Amos's prophecies show signs of careful composition. None was off the top of his head. He had studied the form in which other prophecies had been couched – the poetry, the balance, the refrains, the epigram, the play on words. And he used them all with an eloquence and skill that prove he was no mere yokel.

God's word deserves the finest presentation at any time: prepared, mulled over, with words and sentences chiselled and refined. There is no virtue in casualness or lack of thought. Immediacy there must be, but that is not bought at the price of artistry. The message must get home. A Church which still believes in communicating the gospel needs to be more skilled at the techniques and skills of that craft.

4. Bearing the Consequences

Being faithful to God's word can be very costly. Amos found it so, as did many of the prophets. 'For so men persecuted the prophets who were before you' (Matt. 5.12). It was an inevitable consequence, a mark of genuineness. Fallen humanity cannot bear to hear God's assessment on it without in some way lashing back.

For Amos the reaction came from the established Church, from Amaziah priest of Bethel and chaplain to the royal household of the king of Israel. That in itself is a cautionary tale for all clergy in the Church of England! Can one be a prophet and a man of the institution at one and the same time? Can a national church ever exercise a truly prophetic ministry to its own people, or does prophecy demand a degree of detachment? Amos spoke out – and suffered for it: misrepresentation, derision, rejection. Chapter 7 tells the story, and even though the prophet had the last word it was no pleasant experience to have to bear.

What does Amos have to teach us who live out our suburban lives in twentieth century Britain? Undeniably we are caught up in as many social evils as he was in his day: the drunkenness, the immorality, the grinding of the poor, the sharp practices, the injustices. They still continue, even in a society which is propped up by social security, democratic government and the Ombudsman. So we need the voice of our latter-day Amoses and maybe we have to let them come from the ranks of amateurs, the men with no political axe to grind, no vested church interest to protect. Maybe we need to invite such people to do a 'partners in mission' critique of the Church, and listen carefully to their criticisms of us? We who like to play the Amos ourselves are not above reproach.

To be an Amos, one must be a man who walks and talks with God, with a commitment to him which is matched by a detachment from the world we live in. A detachment, not from its life but from its values and from its downward gravitational pull. One must be informed and educated so that our words are not made to look ridiculous because they are ill-judged and clumsy. Above all, we must be prepared to bear the suffering which a prophet faces when his words strike home.

To be a prophet is not a calling that is embraced lightly. The true prophet is always a reluctant disciple, pressed into service against his will and his better judgement by the insistent call of God. He will be for ever on the battlefield, wrestling with himself as Jeremiah often did, and with those he is called to confront. He may end up a broken man as a result.

Beware the false prophet, who rather enjoys his role and does well out of it, who speaks peace when there is no peace, who is a man of compromise and not a man of the desert. And pray that God will give us the right people to speak his message and bring cleansing and repentance to our land.

Prayer: Lord God, when corruption abounds and Christians grow cynical; when racialism is rampant and Christians seek their own interests; when consciences are stifled and it is safer to keep silent – call out your prophets. Give them courage to speak, charity in doing so, and a fire in the belly, which will not let them be silent: by the power of your Holy Spirit. (A prayer of J. Wheatley Price taken from *Prayers for Today's Church*)

(Hymns: *For the healing of the nations; Lo, in the wilderness a voice; Disposer supreme, and Judge of the earth; Lord, Thy Word abideth.*)

23. 'WHAT SHALL I BRING?'

Micah 6.6 *'With what shall I come before the Lord, and bow myself before God on high?'*

Aim: To teach the need for *being* religious instead of *doing* religion.

There were three questions that were always instilled into me when as a boy I was packed off to church or to Bible class. Have you cleaned your shoes? Have you got a clean handkerchief? And have you any collection? They are a far cry from the Old Testament's demand for clean hands and a pure heart, but that's another story. Micah's question is about the collection and that certainly rings true. With what shall I come before the Lord? What shall I bring? Have I got enough?

If you look more closely at the context you will see that the question is misdirected. God has a controversy, a quarrel, with his people. They have been persistently disobedient; they have ignored his laws, and their religion is no more than skin-deep. They have responded to God's many blessings with total ingratitude and so God appeals to them in the words, 'O my people, what have I done to you? In what have I wearied you? Answer me! For I brought you up from the land of Egypt, and redeemed you from the house of bondage . . . . that you may know the saving acts of the Lord' (6.3–5).

Clearly the call is to repentance, a changed attitude to God. Are there any glimmerings of love or gratitude from his people? They respond instead with a pseudo-repentance. About gifts and compensation. How can they make up for their past failings? With more generous donations to the Church! 'Shall I come before him with burnt offerings, with calves a year old?' That was a sacrifice hallowed by tradition. Maybe that would please God. Or the jumbo gift? 'Will the Lord be pleased with thousands of rams, with ten thousands of rivers of oil?' Surely that would be acceptable and show how much they meant to repent. Or they could go for the ultimate in sacrifice and emulate Abraham in his offering of Isaac. 'Shall I give my first-born for my transgression, the fruit of my body for the sin of my soul?'

God waves it all aside. He is looking for repentance, not for donations. He wants the giver, not the gifts. 'He has showed you, O man, what is good; and what does the Lord require of you but to do justice, and to love kindness, and to walk humbly with your God?' (6.8).

There are many things we can learn from Micah's teaching. The first is the insidious temptation we face to resort to spurious means of appeasing a guilty conscience. We try to buy peace of mind. The lavish gifts a divorced parent gives to his children are just one example of a man trying to hide the guilt of his broken marriage behind a facade of extravagant love and overdone generosity. Shall I give the fruit of my bank account for the sin of my soul? We all do it in a variety of ways: not one of us is guiltless. It's human nature – but that doesn't excuse it either.

Then there is a warning to us here that we must come to God on his terms, not our own. We ask ourselves, 'How can I make my peace with God?' God replies 'You cannot make peace', and the apostle Paul explains 'Therefore, since we are justified by faith, we have peace with God through our Lord Jesus Christ' (Romans 5.1). Christ is our peace and has made peace for us, so that we can enter into that peace and be reconciled to God. Salvation is by grace through faith, but there is something inside us (our old Adam, if you like) that says it would prefer it if we could be saved by works, by something that we had to do ourselves. It is the heresy known as Pelagianism, after a fifth century theologian named Pelagius. Significantly Pelagius was an Englishman, and his heresy lingers on in his descendants. The Englishman is a self-made man, and he worships his creator. . . .

The greatest lesson, however, of this text is to learn what the Lord does require of us – to do justice, to love kindness and to walk humbly with our God. In these three phrases are combined the essentials of true religion as the eighth-centry prophets taught it. Micah's three great contemporaries were Amos, Hosea and Isaiah, and you could say that these three qualities were their three emphases. Justice was Amos's great clarion-call ('Let justice roll down like waters and righeousness like an ever-flowing stream', Amos 5.24). Kindness was at the heart of Hosea's gospel ('I desire kindness/steadfast love and not sacrifice, the knowledge of God, rather than burnt offerings', Hosea 6.6). And humble faith was Isaiah's watchword ('O house of Jacob, come, let us walk in the light of the Lord', Isaiah 2.5). Let us look at these requirements one by one.

1. *Do justice*

Two out of the three things that God requires of us are to do with our fellow men and only one deals with our relationship with God. This in itself tells us something about the importance God attaches to human behaviour. We are to do justice, to be utterly straight in our dealings with our fellow men. There is to be no deviousness, no shadiness, no sharp practice. We are to be transparently honest – in our words, in our business dealings, in financial matters, even in our tax returns.

Doing justice means more than personal integrity however. For the Hebrew, doing *mishpat* meant rightings wrongs and interfering in other people's business for their good. It was not a *laissez faire* policy of non-intervention in politics or in civic affairs. It meant making special efforts to plead the cause of the fatherless and the widow, the one-parent family and the pensioner. It was done not to catch votes but to please God. We still need workers for justice in our society, preferably people who are doing it for the right reason. God requires it of us.

2. Love kindness

The word for 'kindness' is one of the great characteristics of Old Testament religion. It describes the unique love of God, true to his covenant, true to his word, unchanging, unwavering. What Micah is saying in this verse is that God expects his people to love others in just the same kind of way as he loves them. It is a love with a large measure of generosity about it, a big-hearted love, a forgiving love. It is not far removed from the Beatitude, 'Blessed are the merciful for they shall obtain mercy'. It is what St John was looking for when he appealed to his readers: 'Beloved, let us love one another; for love is of God, and he who loves is born of God and knows God . . . . And this commandment we have from him, that he who loves God should love his brother also' (1 John 4.7,21). It is what God requires of us.

3. Walk humbly with God

There is a proper modesty about a man's relationship with his Maker that is not to be found in every Christian's life. The follower of Christ does not put on airs, he puts on humility. He is not arrogant but respectful, not assertive but retiring. He is teachable and readily accepts his dependence upon God. He is a servant of others and does not lord it over them. He walks in

step with God and does not seek to outstrip him or to lag
behind.

One of the hardest lessons the Christian needs to learn is that
what he is matters more than what he does, and that true religion
is a matter of daily living and not of so-called religious exercises
or experiences. What then shall we bring to God? We have
nothing to offer that is fit for him – only our sins to be forgiven
by him, our lives to be surrendered to him, our souls and bodies
to be a living sacrifice for him.

Then and only then can we begin to fulfil his requirements –
to do justice and to love kindness and to walk humbly with our
God.

Prayer: Teach us, good Lord, to serve you as you deserve, to do
your will, to love as you love us and to live submissively
in the light of your presence.

(*Hymns: What does the Lord require for praise and offering?; O for a
closer walk with God; All praise to thee, for thou, O king
divine.*)

24. A FAITH THAT QUESTIONS

Habakkuk 2.4 '*Behold, he whose soul is not upright in him shall fail,
but the righteous shall live by his faith.*'

Aim: To show from a general study of Habakkuk's teaching that
faith is not the unquestioning acceptance of the unbelievable but
a thoughtful exploration of problems in a state of openness to
God.

It was of course from Habakkuk that the apostle Paul quarried the foundation-stone of his great epistle to the Romans in the words 'the just shall live by faith' (Romans 1.17). Quoted and rediscovered by Martin Luther it became the proof-text for the Reformation doctrine of justification by faith alone.

Important as that may be for later church history it will not necessarily help us to get inside the mind of this minor prophet who lived and wrote in the latter part of the seventh century BC, when Jeremiah was making his way to manhood. Habakkuk has left us two compositions – an oracle couched in ponderous poetical form (chapters 1 and 2) and a prayer or psalm which was set to music (chapter 3). Of the man himself we know nothing whatsoever. We can judge him only by what he has written.

The strand that runs through these chapters is the quality of faith, as St Paul accurately observed, but not a meek, submissive faith. Habakkuk was not averse to asking God questions – deep, probing questions like 'How long shall I cry for help, and thou wilt not hear? Or cry to thee "Violence!" and thou wilt not save?" ' (1.2).

1. *Questioning faith*

He could ask questions like those because he knew how to be honest with God. Faith is all about relationships, and a relationship to survive must be real. It cannot cloak itself in petty deceit, it must not act a part. The actor is the one man who cannot get through to God. He is the hypocrite to whom Jesus gave such short shrift.

So, if you believe, you must be honest; and if you are honest you will have questions to ask and doubts to express. Habakkuk had his.

His first question was about God's apparent inactivity in a world of mounting wickedness; 'the law is slacked and justice never goes forth. For the wicked surround the righteous, so justice goes forth perverted.' It was the hoary chestnut about why the wicked prosper and always get away with it and God never seems to intervene. However, the fact that it had been asked before does not prevent Habakkuk from asking it again.

Back comes the answer. 'Look among the nations, and see; wonder and be astounded. For I am doing a work in your days that you would not believe if told. For lo, I am rousing the Chaldeans. . .' (1.5, 6). In terms of political history this means that the Assyrians are due for their come-uppance at the hands of Nabopolassar and the growing might of the Babylonians – as happened in 625 BC when Babylon was liberated and thirteen years later when Nineveh fell and with it the whole Assyrian empire.

Which is marvellous news from one point of view, but it raised for Habakkuk yet another problem. How can a holy God like the Lord use such unholy and idolatrous instruments as the Babylonians to do his will? 'Thou that art of purer eyes than to behold evil and canst not look on wrong, why dost thou look on faithless men?' (1.13).

Now these are real questions that faith cannot turn a blind eye to. They are puzzling, contradictory, problematic. They need to be asked and, if possible, answered. There is no harm in expressing doubts like these. They are doubts that arise from a standpoint of faith, which is very different from the doubt that is really disbelief in question form. A proper living relationship between man and God can stand such dialogue.

2. *Living faith*

Habakkuk was quite prepared for the possibility that his questions would not be answered. Faith asks, then waits and listens. 'I will take my stand to watch, and station myself on the tower, and look forth to see what he will say to me' (2.1). An answer came, but it was not the answer to what had been asked. It was a word from the Lord. Cryptic, profound, lapidary. 'Behold, he whose soul is not upright in him shall fail, but the righteous shall live by his faith.'

Here is our text. It does much more than deal with Habakkuk's immediate problems. It speaks about the nature of a man's inner being, his soul. The man who is not upright, be he Ashurbanipal the Assyrian or Nebuchadrezzar the Chaldean, will crumple and fall. Godlessness has the seed of its own destruction within it. The wicked need never be envied, despite his shortlived success. He should only be pitied – and prayed for.

The righteous on the other hand will enjoy abundance of life through his faith. He will be like the proverbial tree planted by the waterside whose leaf never withers. His faith will be the mainspring of his life, the secret source of all his energy and vitality. This is what our Lord referred to when he said 'He who believes in me, as the scripture has said, "Out of his heart shall flow rivers of living water".' And John adds, 'Now this he said about the Spirit, which those who believed in him were to receive' (John 7.38, 39).

Through such words as these Habakkuk learnt that there was more to the life of faith than having difficult questions answered. If his soul was right with God most of the other issues would fall into place or could be lived with. A personal living faith was primary to all such investigation. That was the message at the heart of Paul's teaching, and it was the message of the Reformation too.

3. *Suffering faith*

In his concluding psalm Habakkuk comes out with a sentence which must surely be the high point in the Old Testament's portrayal of genuine faith. 'Though the fig tree do not blossom, nor fruit be on the vines, the produce of the olive fail and the fields yield no food, the flock be cut off from the fold and there be no herd in the stalls, yet I will rejoice in the Lord, I will joy in the God of my salvation' (3.17,18).

This is like the faith of Job who said of God 'Though he slay me, yet will I trust in him'. It is the faith that goes on trusting when all logic goes on record as saying that it is futile to do so. It is the faith that can smile in the face of suffering, that can survive without the need for props and reassurances.

As the child is helped to grow out of dependence upon a night-light, so the Christian needs to mature into a faith that trusts God come what may. Few of us actually get that far. Fewer still have learnt to believe when all the evidence is positively alien to faith. But that is surely the goal to which we should aspire and to which Habakkuk calls us by his example and by his words.

Prayer: Forgive us, Lord, for the weakness of our faith. May we grow in trust and dependence upon you, sharing our problems with you, waiting patiently for you to reveal yourself, asking for nothing but the knowledge that you are there and that you understand everything and that all is in your hand.

(Hymns: Jesus, I will trust Thee; Jesu, priceless treasure; My faith looks up to Thee.)

25. CONSIDER YOUR WAYS

Haggai 1.2 *'Thus says the Lord of hosts: This people say the time has not yet come to rebuild the house of the Lord.'*

Aim: To encourage a congregation to embark on some project which will demonstrate in practical terms their obedience to God. This could be a stewardship mission, a church restoration programme or even a working-party to spring–clean the church. The theme is that good intentions are not enough. Read in preparation the whole of Haggai 1.

The experienced committee-man knows that if he wants to squash a suggestion he does not approve of, the best way is not to disagree with it but to make a speech generally in support of it; but then to add, with a regretful shake of the head, that it is badly timed and should be reconsidered when a more appropriate moment arises. Group inertia can be relied upon to do the rest.

Inertia was the public enemy confronting the prophet Haggai when he spoke these words. Seventeen years had gone by since the advance party of exiles had returned to Jerusalem filled with enthusiasm to rebuild the city and restore the burned–out temple. They had got as far as putting roofs over their own heads but then the problems of living had begun to occupy their full attention and the temple was left to another day. They had excellent excuses for the delay. It was a 'major task' and needed careful thought and preparation. If it was going to be done at all it must be done well. God's house deserved the best, and the best was not immediately available in a day of economic decline. So nothing was done. The temple continued to be a ruin, a disgrace to Jerusalem and an appalling advertisement for Jerusalem's God.

Then Haggai began to preach. 'Is it a time for you to dwell in your panelled houses, while this house lies in ruins?' he asked (1.4). And he challenged them to consider their ways, to examine themselves and to give honest answers to the searching questions he was about to put.

1. *'What are your priorities?'*

This question goes to the very heart of a man's being. It deter-
mines his decisions, his ambitions, his religion, his way of life.
Many people never consciously work out what their priorities
are in life. Like butterflies they flit from one opportunity to the
next – without a pattern, without any conscious choice. They
experience a lot, they achieve little. But the Christian disciple-
ship to which God calls us is all about priorities and decisions
and saying No to this and Yes to that.

For Haggai's hearers the choice was between their own homes
and the Lord's house. They were a nation of DIY fanatics when
it came to their own houses, with ornamental dadoes, decorative
panelling and the very latest in soft furnishings. But God's house
was a very different story. 'One day we'll get round to it', they
said. But Haggai asked: 'Who comes first? Yourselves or your
Lord?'

2. *'What is the message of the harvest?'*

At first sight this has little relevance for us today because food
production balances itself out across the world and all we notice
is a penny extra here or tuppence there. But in the Bible times
(and it still applies today in the developing countries) the success
or failure of the main crop was a pointer to life or death, survival
or starvation in the ensuing year. The Hebrew believed that a
good harvest was a sign of God's blessing and a bad one was the
reverse. So the godly Hebrew learnt to read something of God's
will by the economic state of the nation.

We may not be so simplistic in our approach to world
economics – and the Bible does not encourage us to be – but we
should be prepared to ask ourselves the question: 'Is God saying
something to us as a nation through our present troubles?' In
Haggai's time the trouble was a series of bad harvests followed
by galloping inflation. 'You have sown much, and harvested
little . . . and he who earns wages earns wages to put them into a
bag with holes' (1.6). We recognize that second part only too
well.

If we can apply any of this to our life today, I think it would be
the fundamental lesson that a time of economic stringency is the
best time to appeal for heroism and true dedication. Just as the
persecuted Church is much more effective than the prosperous

Church, so when the shoe pinches and times are hard the Church is better able to hear the threefold call to self-denial, cross-bearing and following Jesus. Today's prophet, like Haggai, learns to read the signs of the times and to preach accordingly.

3. *'When will you do something?'*

We are back where we began with the problem of inertia. 'This people say the time has not yet come to rebuild the house of the Lord.' The prophet scolded and probed, but at the end of his sermon he called not for a decision couched in the language of prayer but for some action. 'Go up to the hills and bring wood and build the house' (1.8). What refreshing directness! Here is the Bible's insistent reminder that obedience to God is a matter not of so-called 'spiritual exercises' but of practical things like writing a letter, calling on a neighbour, scrubbing a floor, signing a cheque – or going to chop wood!

Very few present-day sermons call for any practical response. Indeed, the pattern of our worship, with the sermon followed by a hymn, the collection, the blessing, the departure of the choir and shaking hands at the door, is hardly conducive to eliciting a practical response from the congregation. Rarely does the preacher expect his hearers to behave differently as a result of his preaching. Perhaps the Sunday service is not the best place for speaking the 'word of prophecy': maybe the church council meeting would be better.

At all events Haggai's preaching did not fall on deaf ears. 'Then Zerubbabel and Joshua the high priest, with all the remnant of the people, obeyed the voice of the Lord their God, and the words of Haggai the prophet, as the Lord their God had sent him; and the people feared before the Lord' (1.12). The reason they did so was because they heard two voices, not one. They heard Haggai's words, challenging, declaiming, questioning; and they also heard the Lord's voice, inwardly, touching heart and conscience, irresistible and inescapable. True prophecy always packs the double punch: a man's words and the Lord's voice. That is why most preachers pray before they go into the pulpit and they probably pray that while they are preaching the sermon that they have so carefully and prayerfully prepared, their hearers may hear that other voice that lodges deep down in the heart.

4. *As man works, so God works*

Encouraged by the success of his preaching, Haggai is inspired to utter another word. A mere seven words in English, four in Hebrew. 'I am with you, says the Lord' (1.13). What does this mean? He is saying that as the people have changed their minds towards God, so God is changing his mind towards them. Of course, it is human language that is being used, and God does not have human emotions. But Haggai wants the people to know without delay that God is on their side, working with them in their new endeavours. He is no longer finding fault, judging, censuring. They have listened to that voice, and now he is encouraging, reassuring, supporting. 'I am with you, says the Lord.' We do not have to go far along the road of penitence and obedience before we find the Father running to meet us with words of welcome and reassurance.

So the chapter ends with the Lord stirring up the spirit of the leaders and the people, so that 'they came and worked in the house of the Lord of hosts, their God'. It was one of the Bible's success stories. Out of it there came the second temple in Jerusalem which was to last for hundreds of years until the days of Herod who refurbished it at enormous expense, and of Jesus who replaced it at even greater expense.

All because a man preached, and a people listened, and did something about it.

Prayer: O God, show us what you want us to do and give us the grace to do it, that we may be doers of the word and not hearers only.

(*Hymns: Soldiers of Christ, arise; Rise up, O men of God; Lord of all power, I give you my will.*)

26. BEGINNING. . .NOW!

Haggai 2.19 '*Is the seed yet in the barn? Do the vine, the fig tree, the pomegranate, and the olive tree still yield nothing? From this day on I will bless you.*'

Aim: To encourage persistence in a given undertaking. This sermon could well follow up the previous one, picking up some of its teaching and assuring the hearers of God's blessing on their work and of his unlimited resources as they tackle it. Read in preparation the whole of Haggai 2.

We know virtually nothing about the prophet Haggai who first spoke these words and there is not much we can infer about him from only two chapters of text. The one thing we do notice about him, however, is that he was a stickler for dates. In the course of less than four months of public ministry he or his chronicler noted down no less than four times the day of the month when the word of the Lord came to him, and two other dates are given a mention as well.

This is how his second chapter begins: 'In the second year of Darius the king, in the seventh month, on the twenty-first day of the month, the word of the Lord came by Haggai the prophet.' This means it was a bare seven weeks since his first recorded sermon had stirred the people to do something about the dilapidated temple in their midst. It was less than a month since the sound of hammers and chisels echoing round Jerusalem had indicated that the working-party was actually on the job. Why, then, did the prophet need to say something more?

The answer is that enthusiasm quickly evaporates. In the case of those rebuilding the temple it was not so much that they did not want to do what they could for God, but that the task seemed so immense. This was particularly true for those with long memories who had some idea of what the temple had originally looked like: the magnificent inlays, the gold fittings, the polished stonework, the elegant murals. In comparison with that, the best they could afford to do was going to look very second-rate and amateur.

Haggai put their thoughts into words 'Who is left among you that saw this house in its former glory? How do you see it now? Is it not in your sight as nothing? But then he added: 'Yet now take courage, O Zerubbabel. . . . take courage, O Joshua . . . take courage all you people of the land, says the Lord; work, for I am with you, says the Lord of hosts.' In point of fact, the second temple turned out to be a very modest building when compared with its predecessor. But as far as Haggai was concerned, there were more important considerations to be borne in mind. For example:

1. *Doing a task is often of more value than completing it*

There is a benefit in working for God which makes the enterprise more worthwhile than the achievement. Work of this kind is a means of grace. As long as we are busily obeying God we are candidates for God's blessing. Many Christian people never seem to learn this lesson. They are content to leave the chores to others and never to take on any responsibility for the life of the church to which they belong. Of course they can say that their daily work is their Christian service; they are busy people and have many other commitments. But a household only hangs together when every member does his share, and the household of God is just the same. The person who works for God demonstrates that belonging to the church is something that matters, and he is blessed as he does his part.

2. *Knowing what God's resources are like is more important than finding one's own*

Far too many churches today are obsessed with problems of fund-raising. There is the quota to pay, the heating bills, the insurance, the repairs to budget for, and woe betide the clergy if they incur any expenses in doing their work for the church! The church treasurer wears a worried look all through the year and says a silent prayer that the grand Christmas bazaar will produce the financial equivalent of a miraculous draught of fishes so that the books can balance and the bills be paid.

I have no hesitation in saying that that kind of financial neurosis is one of the hallmarks of an unspiritual church. The Spirit-filled church on the other hand, though it may have just as many grounds for anxiety, relies upon a God who says 'The silver is mine and the gold is mine' and 'the treasures of all nations shall come in and I will fill this house with splendour' (2.7.8). Yes, God's resources are limitless, and we are on his pay-roll. We have a Rothschild of a God! That is why Jesus could say to his disciples: 'I tell you, do not be anxious about your life, what you shall eat or what you shall drink, nor about your body, what you shall put on. Is not life more than food, and the body than clothing?. . . Your heavenly Father knows that you need them all. But seek first his kingdom and his righteousness and all these things shall be yours as well' (Matthew 6.25,32f.).

3. *What God is about to do is usually better than what he has done*
The future is preferable to the past. Once again, I find that this attitude of mind is rarely reflected in our churches today. All too many of them live on the glories of the past. 'I can remember when the gallery was filled every Sunday morning. If you weren't here twenty minutes before service-time you couldn't get a seat.' You must have heard stories like that as often as I have.

Haggai's words were: 'The latter splendour of this house shall be greater than the former, says the Lord of hosts; and in this place I will give prosperity, says the Lord of hosts' (2.9). Now we have already noticed that from an architectural point of view this did not turn out to be the case, unless you look ahead about five hundred years to Herod's splendid renovation of the temple. Haggai's words did not actually come true during the lifetime of his hearers. One wonders why they were remembered and recorded and passed down to future generations. Surely it was because they stood for a divine principle which Haggai had taught and the people had learnt: that God's future is better than God's past. We must always be looking forward to better things.

Another way of putting this is to say that we live in hope. St Paul frequently wrote about the Christian hope in passages like: 'In hope we were saved. Now hope that is seen is not hope. For who hopes for what he sees? But if we hope for what we do not see, we wait for it with patience' (Romans 8.24f.). Hope is sometimes called a Christian virtue. That is wrong. It is not a virtue; it is a Christian doctrine. Because it stems from the nature of God, who is for ever doing things better.

This leads on to our text. In it Haggai is making reference to the current state of the harvest and is saying that 'from this day on' (another date!) everything is going to change for the better. Why? Look back to the parable of verses 11 to 13. We need not stop over the details of this intricate and archaic piece of legalism, but it gives the Law's judgement that defilement is more contagious than holiness. Then it adds that the whole nation is defiled because of the state the temple has been in and this cannot be remedied merely by the offering of sacrifices. It needs much more radical treatment. It needs the rebuilding programme which the people have just embarked upon. So the stigma will be removed, the defilement will be cleansed and God's blessing will once more come down upon the fruit of the ground. And it will begin at once.

So I say to you, as Haggai said to his hearers: 'Keep up the good work. Do not flag. God's riches are more than enough for all you have to do. Go forward.' And take God's promise with you: 'From this day on I will bless you'.

Prayer: We praise you, O God, for the great things you have done in days gone by. Help us to believe that you can do even greater things, and be with us as we work in your name.

(*Hymns: Go, labour on, spend and be spent; Christ is our corner-stone; Strengthen for service, Lord, the hands.*)

27. 'BY MY SPIRIT'

Zechariah 4.6 '*Then he said to me, "This is the word of the Lord to Zerubbabel: Not by might, nor by power, but by my Spirit, says the Lord of hosts".* '

Aim: To teach the importance of reliance upon God in any human undertaking.

Today's passage is about mountains and molehills. We are familiar with people who have a knack of making out mountains where only molehills are to be found. Every problem is a massive stumbling-block, minor difficulties become major crises, routine decisions take weeks of consultation and measured thought. Life must be very hard work for those with this approach. But for the hero of our text the opposite was proposed. 'What are you, O great mountain? Before Zerubbabel you shall become a plain' (4.7).

Let me sketch in the background. After seventy years of exile in Babylon and fifteen more years of dithering on their return home, the Jewish people were being urged on by Haggai and Zechariah to set to work on rebuilding the ruined temple in Jerusalem. It would restore their self-respect, encourage morale and enable worship to be offered worthily to the Lord who had rescued them out of all their troubles. There was no question in the minds of these two prophets that to rebuild was the will of God, and in this they were supported by the two chief leaders of the community. These were Joshua the high priest (not to be confused with Moses' successor) and Zerubbabel the governor of Judah, who was also incidentally one of the few surviving descendants of the royal line of David and so a man on whom almost messianic hopes were being pinned.

Now the task of rebuilding the temple was no molehill. It was a job of mountainous proportions – quite literally, when you consider the huge pile of rubble that the great temple of Solomon had become in those intervening years since the city had been sacked by Nebuchadnezzar's armies. Zerubbabel had the faith to face up to it; he had more than a dash of optimism in his nature. The people were less convinced. So it was for their benefit as well as the governor's that the word of the Lord came through Zechariah: 'What are you, O great mountain? Before Zerubbabel you shall become a plain'. And again, 'the hands of Zerubbabel have laid the foundation of this house; his hands shall also complete it' (4.9).

How are mountains levelled? How are intractable problems overcome? It is a question to which every Christian leader would like to know the answer. Optimism helps, but it is not enough. In these days of massive earth-moving operations, mountains do get parted with the help of bulldozers, as motorways and railways are constructed through them. But brute strength is not enough either. The lesson God wanted to teach his people through Zechariah was that success in his service is achieved 'not by might nor by power but by his Spirit'.

1. Human Effort

Consider first human effort. Zechariah uses the metaphor of

'the big battalions'. 'Might' and 'power' are both words that can refer to armies or military strength. And it has to be admitted that for a task as huge as converting a mountain of rubble into a temple fit for the Lord, a good case could be made out for bringing in armies of workers, trained, equipped and deployed, and regarding this solely as a test of human resources and organization. It is just possible that it would have succeeded but it would not have been God's way. God was continually anxious that none of his people should ever go around saying, 'My power and the might of my hand have gotten me this wealth' (Deut. 8.17). If they failed to rely on the grace of God for everything, they would be on the slippery slope leading to their own downfall. It was the sin of Adam all over again.

Today's equivalent of 'the big battalions' is our reliance upon church structures, fund raising programmes, recruiting drives and the like, at the expense of prayerfulness, waiting upon God and being open to his Spirit. It is a temptation which is always before us. Because we need to work and plan and organize, it is a small step from using these resources to becoming dependent upon them.

St Paul had to remind us that 'though we live in the world we are not carrying on a worldly war, for the weapons of our warfare are not worldly but have a divine power to destroy strongholds' (2 Cor.10.3f.). It is the same problem as the early Church faced about wisdom and the Gospel, especially when Gnostic wisdom was being put across with such sophistication and persuasiveness; and the Corinthians had to be taught that 'God chose what is foolish in the world to shame the wise, God chose what is weak in the world to shame the strong, God chose what is low and despised in the world, even things that are not, to bring to nothing things that are, so that no human being might boast in the presence of God' (1 Cor.1.27–29).

2. God's Spirit

Reliance upon God's Spirit is a very different thing. It requires four things of us.

(a) That God is the source and inspiration of all our plans. It is always wrong to make plans and then pray for God's blessing upon them. We must be seeking God's will before ever we hatch up our schemes. Only when we are reasonably sure that what we are planning is what God intends should we go ahead in faith.

(b) That there is consensus in the Church. This applies particularly to a costly building project or a daring venture of faith. It is not enough for the Church council to support the vicar in his enthusiasm and vision. The vision must be shared and most people must be in favour. In a fallen world we don't need to wait for unanimity (there will always be one or two dissentients to the best of plans); but the people of God should be convinced by the Spirit of God that this is the will of God.

(c) That the whole undertaking is steeped in prayer, not just as a convention but because we really believe that this is where success in the battle lies.

(d) That we do not succumb to discouragement. Zechariah speaks of those who 'despise the day of small things' (4.10). They may be small achievements, small answers to prayer, or small and insignificant people, but to disregard them as beneath God's notice is sheer stupidity. Some of God's greatest acts have been done through people whom the world would have passed by. Names like William Carey, Gladys Aylward, Mother Theresa, come immediately to mind. It is a comfort to know that God's temple is made up of very small bricks.

3. *The Lampstand*

So finally we turn to the vision of the lampstand in which these words of prophecy are embedded. Most commentators would say that they don't belong to each other at all, and that may have been true in origin. But as they stand in our Bibles they have been put together because someone wanted to say that the prophecy explained the vision. A seven-branched lampstand made of gold is its centrepiece, and the seven lamps are fed from a central bowl or reservoir where olive oil is kept. Either side of the bowl, perhaps embossed on the metal, are two olive trees, symbols of Joshua and Zerubbabel, the two national leaders representing Church and state. The light that shines out from the lampstand (is that a picture of the nation or of the new temple?) comes from the plentiful supply of oil, the oil of God's Spirit. Joshua cannot do it. Zerubbabel cannot do it. Only God can make his people shine as lights in the world, and it is only when we are filled with his Spirit and sensitive to his direction that we shall burn brightly and live effectively for him.

Prayer: Save us, Lord, from relying upon any power but yours, and make us open and obedient to your Holy Spirit.
(*Hymns: Spirit divine, attend our prayers; Have faith in God, my heart; Filled with the Spirit's power, with one accord; We rest on Thee, our Shield and our Defender.*)

28. TRIUMPHAL ENTRY

Zechariah 9.9 *'Rejoice greatly, O daughter of Zion! Shout aloud, O daughter of Jerusalem! Lo, your king comes to you; triumphant and victorious is he, humble and riding on an ass, on a colt the foal of an ass.'*

Aim: To illustrate the style of Christ's kingship in the light of the Cross. The sermon has an obvious bearing on the Palm Sunday narrative.

We cannot read these verses without thinking of their New Testament counterpart. Palm Sunday, the triumphal entry of Christ into Jerusalem, the ride on the donkey, the cries of Hosanna, the cleansing of the Temple. It is a colourful episode that we read with pleasure and satisfaction. The Lord Jesus is getting the welcome he deserves. The common people greet him gladly. The Cross is still a long way away. Ride on, ride on, in majesty! Three cheers for Jesus!

But those who mentally turn it into a royal wedding or a state opening of Parliament are missing the point, just as the Hosanna-shouters did in Jesus' day. They knew their Old Testament a little, but not enough. Enough to see that Jesus was acting the Messiah, but not enough to see what kind of a Messiah he was setting out to be. So, before we are led on by the inexorable flow of the Holy Week story to the cross and passion of our Lord, we pause today and take a long, cool look at the meaning of this Palm Sunday procession as Christ wanted it to be understood.

Undoubtedly the whole incident was planned down to the last detail. The undercover arrangements for acquiring the pair of donkeys are evidence for that. Some may think of this as divine foreknowledge, but it suggests to me rather advance planning with passwords and go-betweens. The whole operation had been carefully set up with a specific purpose and intent – to identify Jesus with the Messiah figure of Zechariah 9. 'Lo, your king comes to you. . .'

1. *A King. . .*

The Messiah had to be a king. All the early expectations were built around David and his descendants, all of them members of Judah's royal house. The day would come when Jerusalem, the city made famous by David, would yet see a king of that royal line entering it in triumph, to usher in the golden age. The idealised picture of a golden past, when David was king and heroes were heroes, became the pipedream of the future. It was a political pipedream of a kind often associated with nations disappointed with their current performance. It was heard in the last American presidential elections. The United Kingdom is not immune ('let's make Britain great once again!') nor Israel, nor a score of other countries. For the people of Old Testament times it was more than merely political, however. It found its origin in God, who was the true King of Israel, whose anointed one would one day demonstrate his reign on earth in Zion, his holy city.

2. *. . . but in humility*

The picture of a king was far from ideal to describe the Messiah's role. Isaiah had spoken about a suffering Servant who would redeem his people through the pathway of rejection, pain and death. Only when the Servant had plumbed the depths of innocent suffering would he be vindicated and reinstated as God's chosen one. But how does one reconcile a reigning monarch and a tortured victim as one and the same Messiah? The Jews found this almost impossible to do and were tempted to settle for two Messiahs, a son of David who would reign for ever, and a son of Joseph who would atone for Israel's sins.

Zechariah drew the two together, so that Jesus could eventually unite them in his person. He said that the coming King was to be 'humble and riding on an ass, on a colt the foal of an ass'. At once we have a picture of modesty and lowliness; no great royal parade but an unassuming, quiet authority. A king who does not glory in his kingliness – any more than his subjects are entitled to do. So, triumphalism is out; meekness is in. A new style of royalty has been born.

3. Prince of Peace

Kings on horseback are associated with battles and warfare. The Messiah however is to be the Prince of Peace. His policy will be disarmament and his gift will be peace for all the nations. Listen to how Zechariah's prophecy continues: 'I will cut off the chariot from Ephraim and the war horse from Jerusalem; and the battle bow shall be cut off, and he shall command peace to the nations'.

It would be attractive to take this prophecy as the Church's official line on nuclear disarmament, but unfortunately the subject is too complex for such simplistic arguments. What is abundantly clear, however, is that every follower of the Prince of Peace must be a man of peace, a campaigner for peace, a believer in peace. That is easier said than done. There is a fatalism around which assumes that the thermonuclear war to end all wars is inevitable and is just round the corner. Young people are heard saying that there's no point in saving for the future, no point in planning for a better world, no point even in being moral, because before long some idiot will press a button and that will be that. Opinion polls give large majorities of those who believe a third world war will come in their lifetime.

Such talk is dangerous and unChristian. The will for peace is the only way to achieving peace, and a fatal resignation is like selling out on a world scale. The Christian must hold to the conviction that Christ is King, the Lord of the destiny of nations, the architect and sustainer of peace. And we are his agents of peace in the world.

4. Ruling the World

When Jesus made his triumphal entry into Jerusalem on that first

Palm Sunday, this was the message he was proclaiming. He was coming not only as Jerusalem's Messiah but as the world's Saviour because, in the words of Zechariah, 'His dominion shall be from sea to sea, and from the River to the ends of the earth.' If he was able to see anything at all beyond the Cross, it was that his mission was for all men everywhere. If he was the Messiah, and if the Messiah was made in Zechariah's mould, then it had to be. He was a King, in humility and peace, and there was no limit to his kingdom.

Few understood. You could hardly expect them to. An excited crowd has no time to read the small print, and all they saw was the well-known prophet of Galilee coming out of hiding and appearing in public in the capital. With our hindsight and with the help of Holy Scripture we can see better what the Lord was trying to say through this meaningful gesture. So we can be more knowing in our Hosannas and in the welcome we offer him, as we say 'Blessed is he who comes in the name of the Lord!'

Prayer: Almighty and everlasting God, who in your tender love towards mankind sent your Son our Saviour Jesus Christ to take upon him our flesh and to suffer death upon the cross: grant that we may follow the example of his patience and humility, and also be made partakers of his resurrection; through Jesus Christ our Lord. (ASB Collect for Palm Sunday)

(*Hymns:* *Ride on, ride on in majesty; All glory, laud, and honour; Christ for the world we sing!*)

29. A WORD FOR THE CLERGY

Malachi 2.4 *'I have sent this command to you, that my convenant with Levi may hold, says the Lord of hosts.'*

Aim: To teach the place of the priesthood within the Church, as indicated by Old Testament expectations of the role of the Levites. Suitable for ordination seasons like Petertide or Michaelmas, but can be used at any time. Read Malachi 2.1–9.

These verses contain the nearest thing that you can find in the Old Testament to a job-description for the clergy. It is not very obvious in our English translation because we do not appreciate what is meant by the phrase 'my covenant with Levi'. But Malachi is writing about the arrangement in the Old Testament community whereby religious leadership was entrusted to the tribe of Levi and their descendants, the Levitical priests. The question before him was 'What are they for?' It takes a prophet to ask such a fundamental question of the religious establishment. This is his answer.

1.   *They are there for the health of the Church*

Verse 5 puts it like this: 'my covenant with him (i.e. Levi) was a covenant of life and peace, and I gave them to him, that he might fear'. The three important words are life, peace and fear, and these are the essential ingredients of the healthy church.

'Life' refers to well-being, activity, potential for growth: it is the opposite of being static and fossilized. 'Peace' is a word that touches on relationships and inner harmony. Where there is peace (*shalom*) all is running smoothly and purposefully. 'Fear' is the sense of reverence that shows itself most of all in the worship of the Church, but is also found as the members respect each other and take seriously their calling to be lights in the world.

How does our Church measure up by these three standards? It is the minister's task to encourage their development. He cannot produce them because they are God's gifts, but he does have the job of facilitating their growth. He is there to enable the Lord's people to be healthy. 'His gifts were that some should be apostles, some prophets, some evangelists, some pastors and teachers, to equip the saints for the work of ministry, for building up the body of Christ' (Ephesians 4.11f.)

2.   *They are there to be an example to the Church*

Read verses 6 and 7 to see what kind of an example the clergy should set. They must be good teachers –'true instruction was in his mouth'. They must give good advice – 'no wrong was found on his lips'. They should be models of personal holiness – 'he walked with me in peace and uprightness'. They should be active in evangelism – 'he turned many from iniquity'.

So the priest is a teacher and counsellor, a man of God and an evangelist. Fortunately, in these days of the New Testament Church the Holy Spirit has distributed his gifts more widely around the congregation so that total omnicompetence is not expected of one man. But anyone who serves in the ordained ministry must ensure that elements at least of these four priestly qualities are found in his ministry and in the corporate life of his congregation.

3. *They can damage the Church if they fail in their task*

That is the message of verse 8. By not keeping to God's ways, by deviating from the path themselves, the priests of Malachi'a day had led others astray and caused many to stumble. 'It is necessary', said Jesus 'that temptations come, but woe to the man by whom the temptation comes!' (Matthew 18.7).

Here is the appalling responsibility of spiritual leadership. The influence for good is so great, but the potential for causing havoc in the Church is just as great. Which leads me to the conclusion that those who are called to the priesthood have to accept a higher standard of commitment, of self-discipline, of morality even, so that they do not lead the faithful away from the way of Christ.

4. *Despite their failures, God still intends to use them in his service*

Here we come to the actual words of our text – 'that my covenant with Levi may hold'. If the covenant with Levi means God's gift to his Church of the ministry, as I believe it does, this is Malachi's way of saying that God has not discarded this plan. He wants it to hold, to be a success, to fulfil his intentions. He is committed to it as the right way forward.

The ministry means a variety of things. To some it means an unbroken succession of orders from the time of the apostles down to the present day. To some it means a threefold ministry of bishops, priests and deacons, which can certainly not be traced right back to New Testament origins but has served the Church well over the majority of her life. To others it means the spiritual principle that God never leaves his flock without shepherds, men or women who are called and trained and commissioned for the task of feeding and caring for the sheep. The important point is that the Church *needs* the ministry, and depends on her ministers for life and health and growth.

And for those who are called to this heavy responsibility Malachi would want to add this footnote, drawn from the wording of verse 2. 'Listen . . . lay it to heart to give glory to my name'. Failure to pay attention to this advice brings disaster. The man who succeeds in his calling to pastor God's people is the man who is for ever attentive to the word of God and to the glory of God. He listens to God rather than the advice of men; he is concerned for God's glory and not for fame and reputation for himself.

It is of such obedience and such humility that good ministers are made.

> Jesus, confirm my heart's desire
> > To work and speak and think for thee;
> Still let me guard the holy fire
> > And still stir up the gift in me.

Prayer: Grant, Lord, to all whom you have called to the sacred ministry of your Church such a sense of their high calling that they may count no sacrifice too great to make in your service; that so, bringing a blessing to their people, they may themselves be blessed by you.

(*Hymns: O Thou, who camest from above; O Thou who makest souls to shine; May the mind of Christ my Saviour.*)

30. THE WINDOWS OF HEAVEN

Malachi 3.10 *'Bring the full tithes into the storehouse, that there may be food in my house; and thereby put me to the test, says the*

Lord of hosts, if I will not open the widows of heaven for you and pour down for you an overflowing blessing.'

Aim: To teach the importance of proportionate giving as of the essence of Christian stewardship. This can be used on Stewardship Sunday or in preparation for a stewardship mission, but it should not be restricted to such occasions.

The Old Testament prophets did not teach the importance of giving. They assumed it. It was an integral part of everyday religion to give one tenth of all income to God. It would have been unthinkable not to. Only in days of marked spiritual decline was the habit not practised, and Malachi's day was one.

What lay behind it? The Israelite believed that increase of every kind was the gift of God and belonged to God. The fruit of his body, the fruit of his fields, the fruit of his cattle, the fruit of his labour. A child, a harvest, a calf, a commercial gain: it was all of God's goodness and must be given back to God in gratitude. So the devout Isaelite gave back the first fruits and a tenth of all his produce, as a reminder that the rest was God's as well – but was given to him by a bountiful God to use and to enjoy. He did not regard it as generosity to be giving God his due: it was simply the right thing to do. He had always been accustomed to living on ninety per cent of his income.

Malachi lived in a time of raging inflation, when people think twice about what they do with their money. And God's work suffered as a result. Malachi takes up the message. 'I the Lord do not change; and you do not cease to be sons of Jacob.' The word for Jacob is like the word for a heel, and Malachi was saying 'Heel by name, and heel by nature'. Just as you tried to do down your brother Esau, so you are trying to do me out of my entitlement. You really are sons of your father Jacob. 'Return to me, and I will return to you.'

Here then is the context in which the prophet calls for a return to a proper standard of giving to God.

1. *Give as a mark of true repentance*
'How shall we return?' ask the people. 'Give evidence that you are coming back to God from your period of backsliding, and start to obey God's laws one by one', replies Malachi, 'beginning

with paying your tithes'. Now no man can buy his way into the kingdom of God, but at the same time no one can say, 'I repent of my sins', without doing something to show that he means it.

Systematic giving is part of the small print on man's contract of obedience to God. It is easy to go out of church saying, 'Through him we offer you our souls and bodies to be a living sacrifice', but what is called for is a detailed outworking of that self-offering – in the way we use our time, how we practise our faith, what we do with our money and how we speak to the traffic warden. Start by paying God what you owe him, is Malachi's advice.

2. *Not to give is like robbing God*

My father has always been a stickler for paying bills immediately. As soon as you get a bill, he would say to me, you are in debt. And every day you don't pay it, you are taking from that man the money that rightly belongs to him.

Malachi would have said much the same. The tenth belongs to God, a debt of honour to be paid. Delay paying it and you are guilty of dishonesty. Refuse to pay it and you are guilty of theft, because you have in your possession goods which belong to someone else.

We sometimes read the parable of the unmerciful servant in Matthew 18 and smile at the unreality of a man owing his master ten thousand talents. But if our own indebtedness to God was added up, in terms of the amount we should have handed over to him and have failed to do, would it not come close to figures like that?

3. *Give a proportion and do it handsomely*

The Jew gave ten per cent and lived on ninety. Only when he had paid that over could he begin to show generosity and give charitably. Tithes were compulsory, offerings were voluntary. We have to work out our own rules for giving – before or after tax, and what percentage it should be – but the important thing is that we give as much as we can, rather than as little as we can, and that we give a proportion rather than a fixed sum, so that our giving will increase as inflation or promotion increases our income.

The bulk of our giving will go to the Church, to maintaining

Christian mission and ministry, and for the relief of hunger and poverty ('that there may be food in my house', 3.10). The allocation of our giving calls for orderliness, discipline and a cash-book!

4. *The more you give, the more you receive*

The Lord's challenge to put him to the test shows the paradox of giving and receiving. We may give to God, and give sacrificially, but he always ensures that we get back more than we give away. It is one of the strange things about giving, and many have testified to the sense of plenty that they enjoy when they plan their giving on generous and biblical lines. There is a revealing phrase found in the Hebrew text of verse 10 and translated in RSV by the one word 'overflowing'. It consists of three short words in Hebrew linked with hyphens and meaning literally 'until-no-need'.

Yes, God's response to our giving is that he will pour out upon us a blessing until we say we have no more need of anything further. Imagine what it would be like for a missionary society to publicize the fact that it has no needs, no shortage of funds, because God's people have paid their tithes in full and the storehouses are packed with the resources required. Yet, that is what should be happening if the Church gives as it has been commanded to give.

Perhaps the fault lies in the fact that we have not 'returned to the Lord', and our commitment to Christ is still only partial. It is in the heart of man that Christian stewardship begins.

Prayer: Help us, Lord, to be good stewards of all that you have given us. May we keep back nothing that we owe you, give generously and cheerfully what belongs to you, and find all our needs met through the riches that are in Christ Jesus.

(*Hymns: Take my life and let it be; Lord of all power, I give you my will; O Lord of heaven and earth and sea.*)